Saltwater Fishing in Washington

by

Frank Haw/Raymond M. Buckley

EDITOR AND PUBLISHER: Saltwater Fishing in Washington is edited and published by Stanley N. Jones. Business office is 3421 E. Mercer St., Seattle, Washington 98102, phone (206) 323-3970.

ART DIRECTOR: Diana Fairbanks.

A Washington State Fishing Guide

preface

The more a person knows about the marine environment and its vast assortment of creatures, apart from the benefits of catching more fish, the better he is able to enjoy an outing. An experience that is completely insignificant to a neophyte could be a never-to-be forgotten event to an informed angler. For example, some Seattle fishermen recently caught what they believed to be a dogfish shark; had some experienced fishermen not informed them that their catch was in fact a sturgeon — a rare catch in salt water — their outing would have been largely wasted.

If this book helps make salt water fishing and more enjoyable for more residents and visitors to Washington, then we will have accomplished our goal. We have tried to present our material in a manner that is helpful to the occasional angler as well as the angler-naturalist. Our use of color photographs of live fish is based on the belief that this is the best method of fish identification for most people. With a few exceptions, the family and species descriptions are short and general to avoid repetition of the detailed information available in scientific texts. In dealing with fishing methods, gear, and bait, we have confined ourselves to those types that we know to be the most effective and pleasing to the angler.

acknowledgements

The maps and text on fishing areas may be the most important part of this book and can be found in no other text. They represent knowledge we have gained over the years during countless successful (and some unsuccessful) fishing trips. A few of the locations can be attributed to our colleagues and friends. We have included the notes on access sites to fishing areas even with the risk they may become obsolete.

Full credit must be given to Nick Pasquale for authorship and the examples comprising the section on filleting, skinning, and steaking the catch. Nick, a fellow biologist and close friend, is considered among his peers to be one of the best in knowing how to prepare fish for cooking.

We are grateful to Don Winsor, Art Director for the Washington State Department of Printing, for his special effort on all of the fishing gear diagrams, and to Nancy Buckley for the artistic sketches that give the finishing touch to the layout of the text. We are also grateful to an unknown artist for the charcoal sketch of the old-timer with the chinook used on the frontispiece. We thank fellow angler-biologist Russ Orrell for much of the information on salmon angling in Saratoga Passage and among the San Juan Islands; and Hugh Statford, photographer, who took the excellent black and white pictures on filleting, skinning, and steaking. Except where noted, the other photos are the authors'. We are also indebted to the Washington Council of Skin Diving Clubs, Inc. (WCSDC), as a source of maximum weights of some local fishes. The Washington Department of Game has provided similar records on the maximum weights of sport- caught trout.

Frank Haw
Raymond M. Buckley

THIS BOOK IS DEDICATED to all those who appreciate our marvelous unspoiled coast, with all its life, and especially to Clinton (Clint) Burt and A. D. (Al) Wells, who are missed.

table of contents

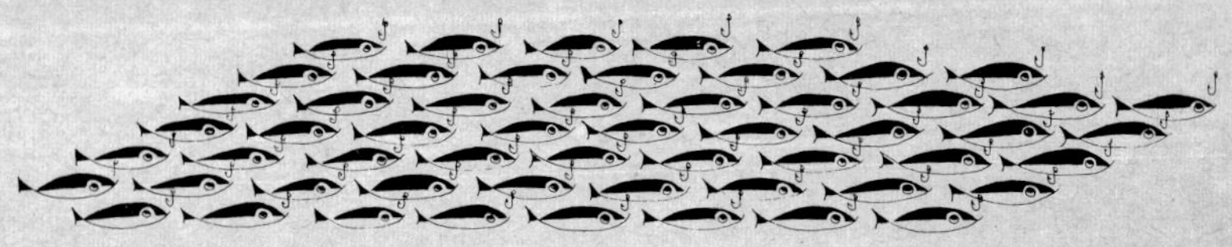

Salmon Hook
(Iron Point)

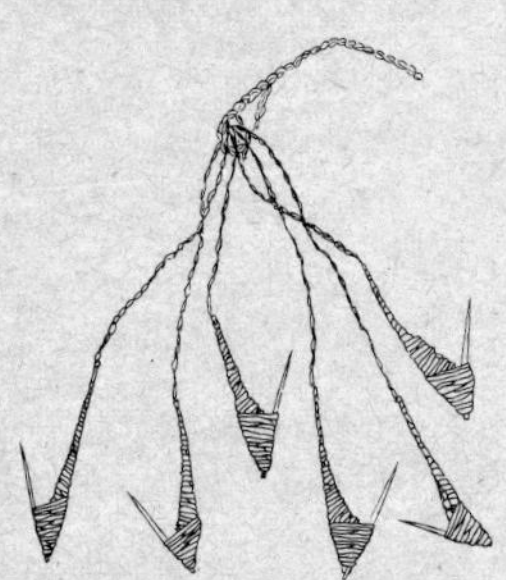

Nootka trolling hooks for baiting whole herring.

introduction

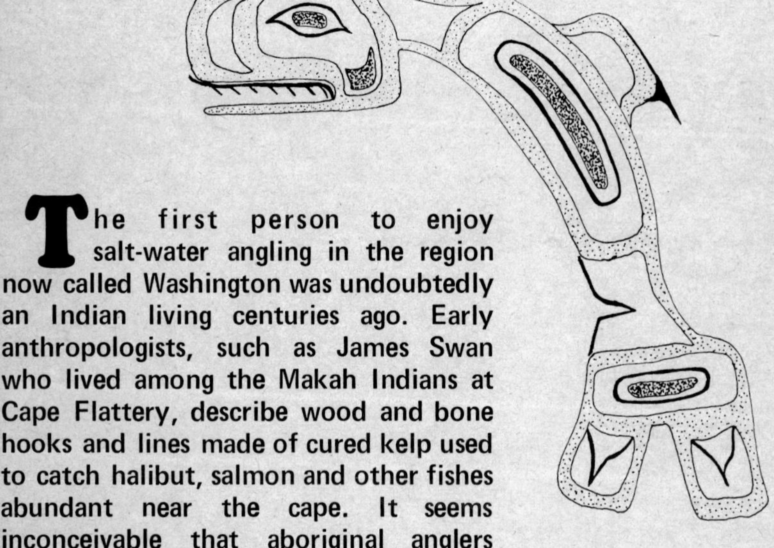

The first person to enjoy salt-water angling in the region now called Washington was undoubtedly an Indian living centuries ago. Early anthropologists, such as James Swan who lived among the Makah Indians at Cape Flattery, describe wood and bone hooks and lines made of cured kelp used to catch halibut, salmon and other fishes abundant near the cape. It seems inconceivable that aboriginal anglers were never thrilled by a leaping salmon or a powerful halibut, testing hand fashioned gear, or that none of these anglers ever caught a fish primarily for fun. Local Indians were so adept at catching salmon on hook and line that they were employed, in the 1850's, by white businessmen to supply the first commercial salmon enterprises on Puget Sound. These businesses were located at the prime fishing areas of Elliott Bay and later at Mukilteo.

The waters of Puget Sound were first charted in the spring of 1792 under the leadership of Captain George Vancouver of the British Royal Navy. Their journals briefly mention hook and line fishing in local waters, but beach seining was the principal method employed by the hungry explorers. The best account concerns fishing on Discovery Bay, located just west of Port Townsend. From descriptions in the journals, it appears that Vancouver's men seined the same species that are still common in the bay. The Captain was especially fond of some small, yellow-green "eels", probably gunnels or blennies, but their efforts did not produce enough to adequately feed the men.

Private Silas Goodrich, who was with Lewis and Clark, may have been the first avid angler to visit our coast. Meriwether Lewis, impressed with Goodrich's catches of black spotted trout and other species, described him as being "remarkably fond of fishing". Salmo clarki (cutthroat trout) were later named after the co-leader who would have been as well remembered without the honor. Perhaps it would have been as fitting if this fine western game fish was named after Goodrich the angler.

After descending the Columbia in the fall of 1805, the members of the Lewis and Clark expedition spent a dreary, wet winter near the ocean. This is no season for fishing here, but along the way even the dying and decaying salmon must have fascinated Goodrich. During the long winter nights, as the gales were blowing the crests from the breakers on the Columbia River Bar, he must have thought of how prime ocean salmon might appear or how they would feel on the end of a line. Perhaps some winter fishing might have saved Goodrich from the discomforts of a disease "contracted from an amorous contact with a Chinook damsel" (Lewis).

The history of Washington's salt-water sport fishery is one of salmon. In 1889, the year the Washington Territory became a state, trolling with spoons was popular on Seattle's Elliott Bay. By 1910, some enterprising salmon anglers fishing from piers along the Seattle waterfront had developed a technique for cutting and rigging herring baits so that they spun when retrieved. Salmon angling bag and size limits were established in 1921 (Minimum length 6 inches; three salmon over 15 inches and 25 between 6 and 15 inches) and by 1931, the boathouse era was well underway with some 2,600 rowboats for hire on the sound. Along with the boathouses came the salmon derbies – and big ones. The Seattle Times derby alone awarded several new cars annually to local anglers. In 1938, the Department of Fisheries began making sport catch estimates when approximately 200,000 salmon were taken by Puget Sound anglers.

The number of rental boats on the sound increased to 3,300 by 1952, but changes were underway: Fishing became popular on western Juan de Fuca Strait, anglers by the thousands were buying their own boats and trailers, sportsmen discovered the salmon and dangers of the open Pacific, and the charter boat industry was born. The boathouse era was ending by the late 1950's and it was suddenly difficult to believe that fishermen by the thousands once rowed from the mainland, through the tide rips, to the southern tip of Whidbey Island and that there were once 152 boathouses and resorts inside of Cape Flattery renting boats to salmon anglers. With the boathouses went the gathering places where, amid a warm atmosphere scented with drying boat cushions, important events were told, retold, and fabricated. This was where a man's reputation as a fisherman was established and recognized and these social functions of the old boathouses have yet to be replaced. By the mid-1960's, although fishing on Puget Sound had suffered, the Washington salmon sport catch was bolstered by ocean fishing and it exceeded a million fish. This was more than the combined sport catches of salmon from the remainder of the North American Coast.

Talking about fishing is an important part of the game, especially valued by old-timers. We enjoy the stories of the old days but we have learned to accept them with reservation. Anglers tend to forget the "skunkings", remember the good trips and the fish tend to grow through the years. One seldom hears of a small fish, yet we know in 1922 such a furor arose when the salmon size limit was raised from six to eighteen inches, that it was immediately lowered to ten inches. And there was the elderly gentleman on the banks of the Deschutes River near Olympia viewing the big mature chinook. He agreed that it was an impressive sight, but then came the inevitable "you should have seen them here in the old days". Rarely is an old-timer trapped, but there were no salmon in the Deschutes in the old days. The falls at the mouth of the river (made famous by a local beer) were impassable until laddered in 1948 for salmon that were stocked.

Civilization has, however, damaged the environment and fishing and it is not what it was in the old days. Using good modern tackle, boats and motors, our best fishermen would have trouble making expenses if they could sell their salmon catch from Elliott Bay or Mukilteo. Even though the mention of Mission Bar, Point Defiance, Possession Point and other Puget Sound fishing sites has lost much of its former magic, there are still many places to fish and many fish to be caught. A few good anglers today on Discovery Bay might catch enough fish to feed a crew the size of Vancouver's and if we could bring Silas Goodrich back for a day in August, he would no doubt have a marvelous time off the mouth of the Columbia. Perhaps the greatest potential lies with the fishes we have overlooked and the fact that a new era is about to begin. The salmon will still be there, but fishermen will discover the other good fishes the Washington Coast has to offer.

As any local swimmer knows, the coastal waters of Washington are cold. During the course of a year, the surface temperatures of Puget Sound at Seattle can be expected to range between 46 and 57 degrees F. Except for salmon, the well-known salt-water sport fish prefer warmer water. Although the number of different species in our cool waters tends to be fewer than occurs elsewhere, what is lacking in variety tends to be made up for in abundance. It is unfortunate that salmon have so completely overshadowed our other species which are on a par with some of the fishes coveted elsewhere. Already, in fact, many of the fishes we overlook are highly valued by California anglers and other fishermen. We have often thought, after encountering a mass of surface feeding black rockfish along the kelp lined shores of Juan de Fuca Strait, that if a black bass fisherman could cast his plug to these frenzied fish it might be difficult for him to go back to his old ways.

— Frank Haw/Ray Buckley —

salt-water fishes important to washington

The beginning pages of almost any fish book include labeled diagrams of fish. Although our approach emphasizes natural color and body form, we must concede that fish identification is simpler if one knows and uses the names of a few anatomical structures. Usually our attempts to identify a fish from a description of a curious angler, who is unfamiliar with basic fish anatomy, has been mutually frustrating. We do remember one successful telephone conversation with an excited woman. She told of catching a very strange fish:

"It was the size and shape of a throw-rug, but it had legs!"

In this case the description was adequate. The lady had obviously caught a large male skate. The

anglers

"legs" were simply large paired male reproductive organs or claspers.

A fish's fins are an obvious part of its anatomy and are very useful in identification. The pelvic (ventral) and pectoral fins are paired, meaning there is one of each on the left and right side. Pectoral fins correspond to the front legs in higher vertebrates (the arms in man) and the ventral fins the rear legs (man's legs). The other fins (dorsal, caudal, and anal) are located along the midline of the fish and are not paired even though they may be subdivided into two or more separate structures, one in back of the other. Fin rays are the structures that support fin membranes. They may be hard with sharp pointed ends (spiny) or they may be soft and branched at the fin's outer edge.

salmon anatomy figure 1

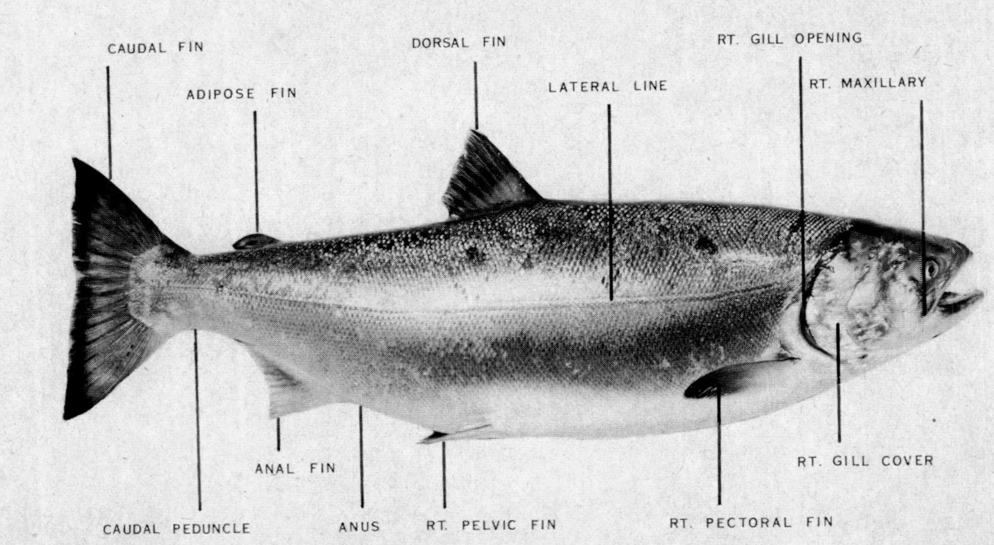

salmon anatomy

(Figure 1)

Salmon are typical of fish with only soft fin rays. They also have a fin with no rays — the adipose (fatty) fin. Skeletal structures of soft rayed fishes tend to be much softer than in fishes with spiny fin rays and the former are considered more primitive.

Hatchery salmon and trout are frequently fin-clipped for latter identification in the wild. Also, the maxillary bones may be clipped. To accurately report a marked fish, one must examine all of these structures for multiple fin marks and be able to distinguish a fish's right from its left.

rockfish anatomy

(Figure 2)

Rockfish are typical of fish with both spiny and soft fin rays. Although the dorsal fin of the rockfish is deeply "notched", it is a single continuous fin. Other fishes, such as cods and some sculpins, have more than one dorsal fin. These are called, beginning with the fin furthest forward, the first, second, or even the third dorsal fin.

flounder anatomy

(Figure 3)

Flounders also have both spiny and soft fin rays, but because of their unusual shape and "blind" side, their anatomy is more confusing. A flounder's mouth slants back toward its belly. The pelvic fins are located on the abrupt ridge of the belly and the anus (remarkably far forward) is just in front of the long anal fin.

rockfish anatomy figure 2

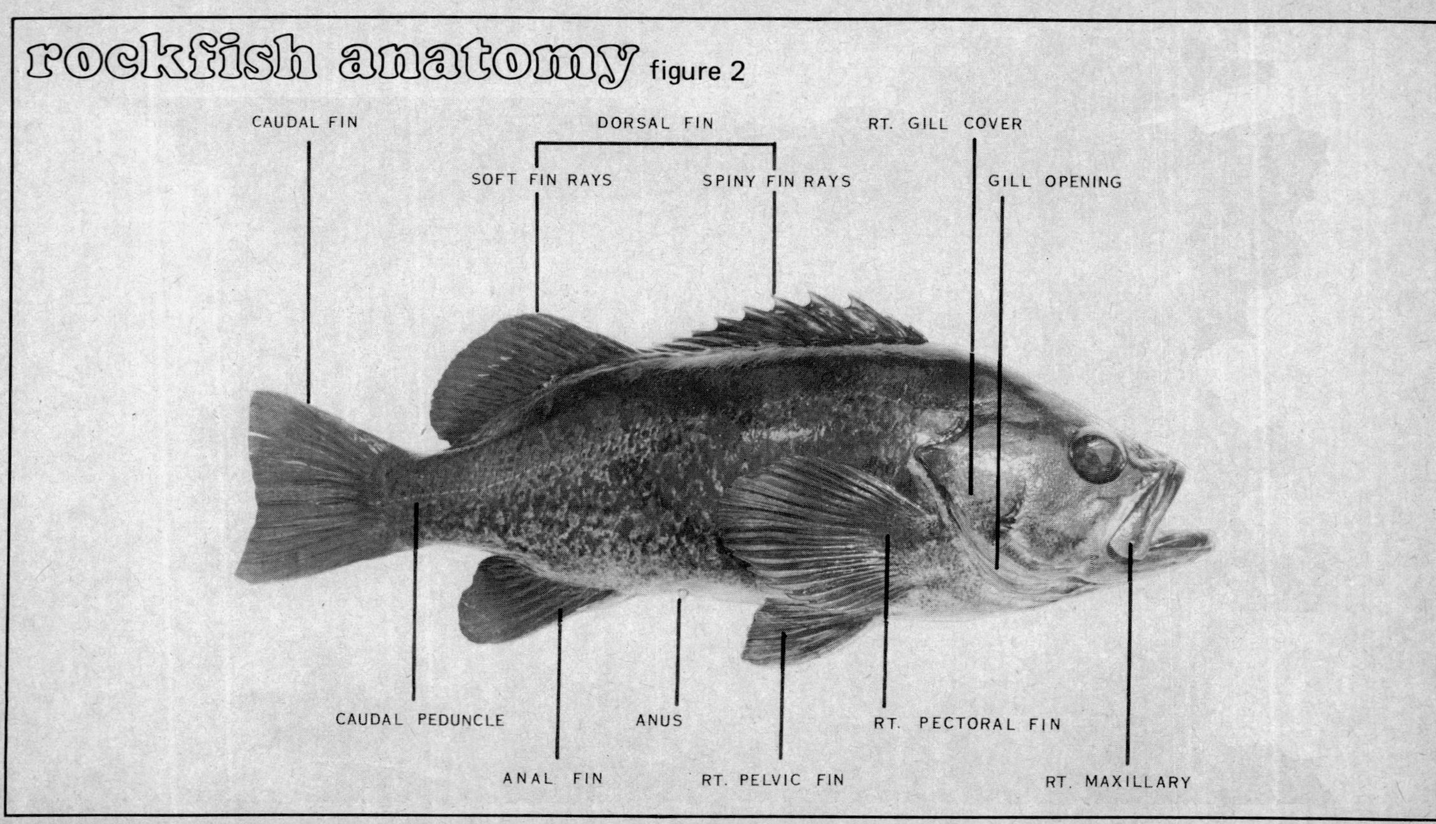

flounder anatomy figure 3

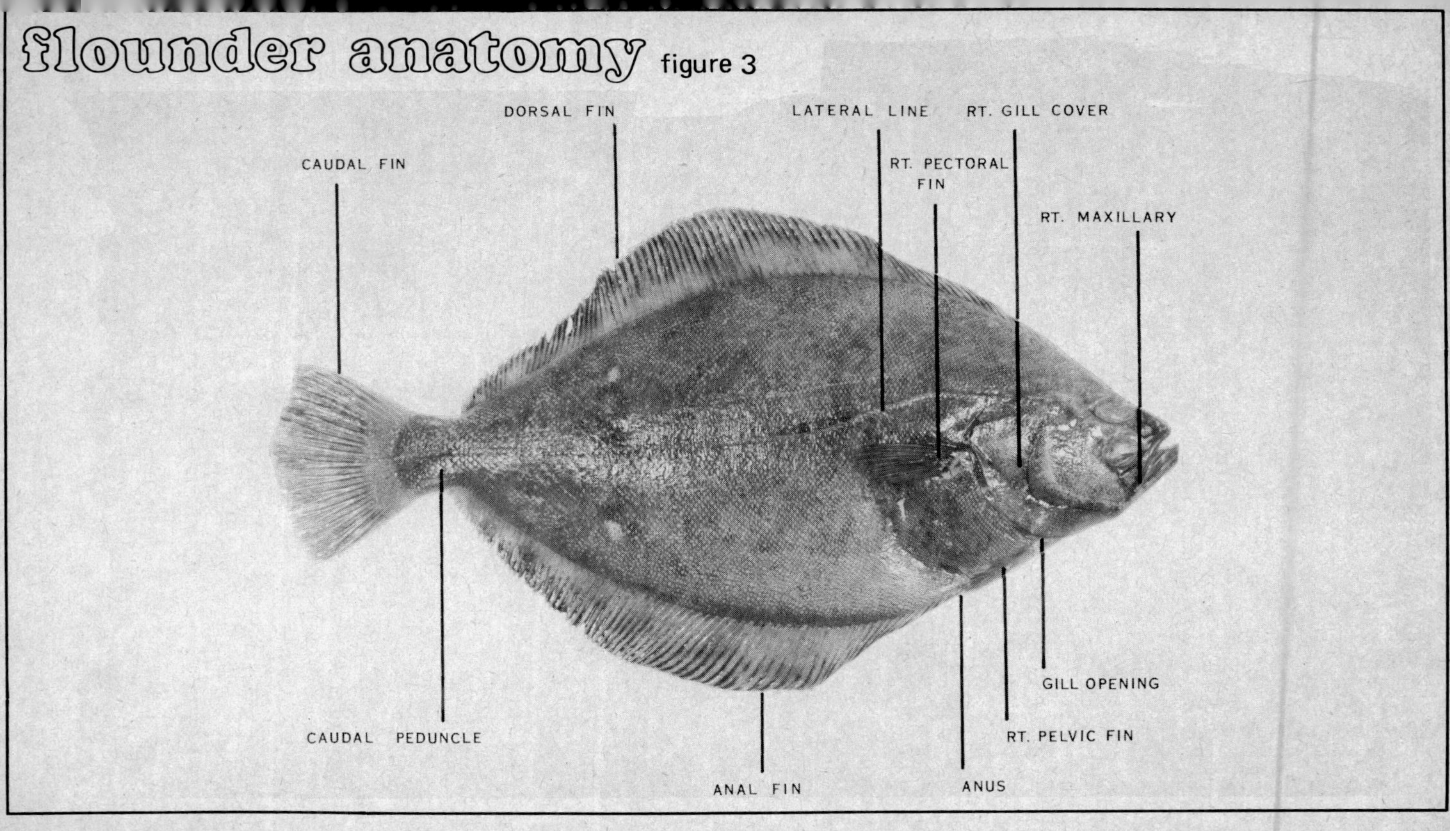

most frequently caught
marine fishes

Fifty-one species of fish, about a sixth of those inhabiting Washington's coastal waters, are pictured in the following pages. These fish are about the only ones an angler can expect to hook in a lifetime of angling in the marine waters of Washington. However, we have omitted entire local families, such as the eel-like pricklebacks (Stichaeidae) and eelpouts (Zoarcidae); or the fascinating pipefish (Syngnathidae), featuring a male that carries the young in a pouch. All the families that we have considered, except the Salmonidae, are only partially represented. The species not included either inhabit the depths beyond the range of sport gear, don't bite, are too small to be hooked, or they are rare. Occasionally, a popular sport fish from the south appears in our cool waters. Bonito have been taken in Puget Sound salmon nets and white seabass have been hooked off Ilwaco and Westport. Recently a large striped bass was taken off Whidbey Island, but all of these fishes are rare and usually appear in late summer or fall when our water temperatures are warmest.

Since natural color and body form are often distorted in death, mostly live specimens were photographed. The common and scientific names used are those recommended in American Fisheries Society Special Publication No. 2, 1960, "A List of Common and Scientific Names of Fishes from the United States and Canada". In addition to these recommended names, a variety of others are included under "aliases". In many cases aliases are frequently used misnomers – some of the most inappropriate are enclosed in quotation marks.

SHARKS (Squaliformes)

The typical shark form is familiar to most anglers: an elongate body that is round in cross-section, fleshy fins that are not collapsible, several gill openings, a mouth located on the underside of the head, and a caudal fin with the upper half larger than the lower half; although in the faster swimming sharks, these lobes of the tail are more uniform. Shark eggs are fertilized internally and male sharks can be easily recognized by their prominent claspers used in copulation.

Although a number of different sharks occur in our waters, only the spiny dogfish is taken frequently. A few others, such as the blue and soupfin sharks, are occasionally hooked by salmon anglers along the outer coast. The sixgill (mud) shark, reported (elsewhere) to reach a length of 26 feet, was taken rather frequently on dogfish set lines from inner Puget Sound when this commercial fishery flourished. These giants are still in the depths of the sound and can be taken on a line baited with a dogfish or some other large morsel. Basking sharks, reported (elsewhere) to reach lengths to 45 feet, have been observed in Puget Sound. Even the notorious white shark ("man-eater") occurs in local waters, although there has never been a known shark attack in Washington.

SPINY DOGFISH (Squalus acanthias) (Figure 1)

Aliases: Dogfish, "sand shark", "mud shark".

Habitat: Very abundant in sand and mud bottom areas throughout Puget Sound, but taken less frequently by coastal and Juan de Fuca Strait anglers.

Baits: Herring and other fishes – an indiscriminate feeder.

Table value: Occasionally tolerated by a few liberal Washingtonians. The flesh should be soaked overnight in a weak acid solution (a little vinegar or lemon juice in water) to remove the urea.

Figure 1, Spiny Dogfish

Most salt-water anglers are contemptuously familiar with this shark. In the past, they have been utilized as sources of sandpaper (skins), with oil and vitamin A extracted from the livers. A frayed, hookless leader is usually indication of a dogfish bite and it is wise to re-tie a hook after a dogfish bites a nylon leader. Nevertheless, introductions to dogfish have thrilled many novice salt-water anglers. The forward edges of both dorsal fins have sharp spines capable of inflicting painful and slightly venomous wounds. The WCSDC* record is 13 lb. 14 oz.

SKATE FAMILY (Rajidae)

Skates are closely related to sharks. They have skeletons of cartilage, several gill openings, a shark-like skin, their eggs are fertilized internally and the males have prominent claspers. Skates, however, are flat but not in the same manner as flounders; skates lie on their bellies, but flounders lie on their sides. Skate "wings" are actually modified pectoral fins. Skates are harmless, although some people confuse them with stingrays (a related fish having a dangerous spine near their tail) that are not found in Washington. However, a few electric rays have been taken from our waters by commercial trawlers from deep water.

SKATES (Raja sp.) (Figure 2)

Alias: "Sting ray"

Habitat: Common on muddy bottomed and in some sandy areas.

Baits: Herring, clams.

Table value: Skate "wings" are highly valued in Europe and by Oriental Americans. The wings are cut from the body, the dark side skinned, then cut into pieces and either boiled or fried. When fried, the meat resembles scallop in taste and texture.

Washington anglers are likely to encounter three kinds of skates: big, long nose, and the starry skate (pictured here). Skates are unimpressive when hooked. They are not uncommon in catches from the ocean surf. The WCSDC record for big skate is 78 pounds 6 ounces, but they are known to attain weights of 200 pounds.

See next page.

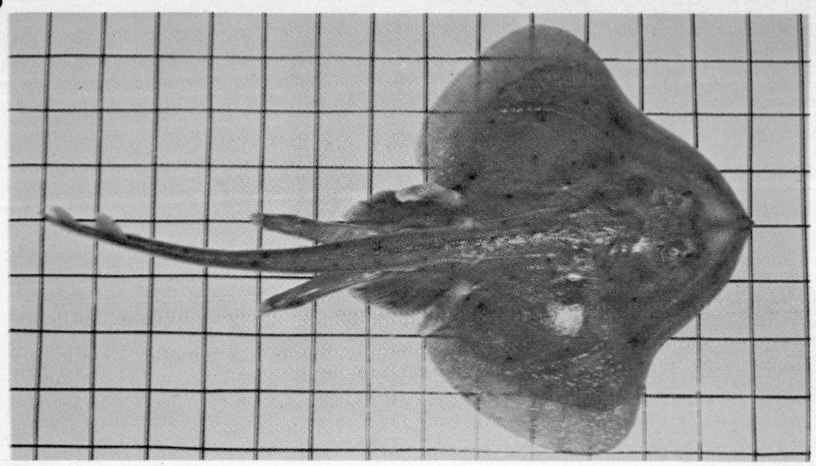

Figure 2, Stary Skate See previous page.

CHIMAERA FAMILY (Chimaerdae)

The chimaeras are similar to the sharks and skates in having skeletons of cartilage, fins that are not collapsible, eggs that are internally fertilized, and males with claspers. They differ in having a single gill opening, a smooth skin, and a body tapering back to a pointed tail.

RATFISH (Hydrolagus colliei) (Figure 3)

Alias: Chimaera.

Habitat: Commonly taken from sandy bottomed areas in depths over 70 feet in Puget Sound and Juan de Fuca Strait.

Baits: Most appear to be taken on herring, but there may be more effective baits.

Table value: Poor.

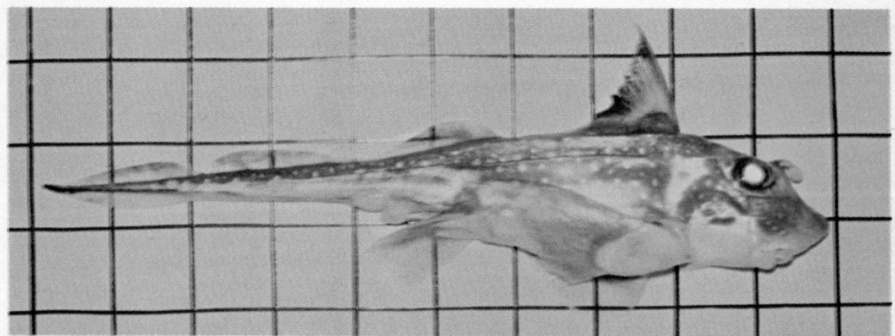

Figure 3, Ratfish

If nothing else, the appearance of a hooked ratfish provides a bizarre interlude to an outing. The forward edge of the first dorsal fin has a sharp spine capable of inflicting a painful and venomous wound. The specimen pictured is a male and differs externally from the female in possessing the head "horn" as well as claspers. Anglers outside the Pacific Northwest seldom see a chimaera. A fine odorless lubricating oil for saltwater reels, guns, and other equipment can be simply rendered from ratfish livers by placing them in a pan in a warm oven. This oil can then be poured off into a container for future use.

STURGEON FAMILY (Acipenseridae)

These are primitive fishes and shark-like in appearance. The upper half of their tail is longer than the lower half and the mouth is located on the underside of the head. Sturgeon differ from sharks in having a sucker-like toothless mouth preceded by a row of four barbels ("whiskers"), a single gill opening, and five rows of bony plates protecting their body.

Sturgeon are slow growing, long lived, and by far the largest local fishes occurring in fresh water. Both our local species also occur in salt water but as with other members of the family, spawning occurs in fresh water. Sturgeon (Huso huso), weighing 2,700 pounds, have been taken in Russia.

WHITE STURGEON (Acipenser transmontanus)

Alias: Sturgeon

Habitat: Frequents the bottom of the deeper pools and channels of the Columbia, Snake, Chehalis, and lower Naselle Rivers. Apparently avoids artificial reservoirs. Occasionally taken from other large coastal and Puget Sound streams. Wide spread but uncommon in the ocean and Puget Sound waters where they are occasionally taken in deep fishing nets.

Baits: Smelt, herring, larval lampreys, night crawlers.

Table value: Excellent.

A white sturgeon taken from salt water by a local angler is a rarity. A specimen weighing 1,285 lbs. was taken from the Columbia River at Vancouver in 1912. An 1,800 pounder has been reported from the Fraser River.

GREEN STURGEON (Acipenser medirostris)

Alias: Sturgeon

Habitat: Principally a salt-water fish that is locally most common near and in the lower estuaries of the Columbia River and in Grays Harbor and Willapa Bay. During periods of high run-off, green sturgeon appear to move away from the river mouths. These sturgeon apparently spend little time in fresh water and ascend rivers only a short distance to spawn.

Baits: Ghost shrimp, crabs, clams, and small flounders have been found in the stomachs of green sturgeon. Herring and smelt should also work.

Table value: Excellent smoked although inferior to fresh white sturgeon.

Anglers, fishing on the bottom with proper bait, should be able to take green sturgeon consistently from Grays Harbor and Willapa Bay during the summer and early fall. Occasionally one is taken by a salmon angler using herring bait. Greens reach a weight of about 350 lbs.

Our two sturgeon species can be distinguished by the bands of olive green running the length of the green sturgeon's body, whereas whites tend to be gray above and white below. In addition, greens have 30 or fewer bony plates in the row extending along the middle of their side, in contrast to a white's 38 or more.

HERRING FAMILY (Clupeidae)

Members of this family, which includes the sardines, are of great importance to anglers as bait and forage for sport fish but one 'herring", the American shad, is itself a splendid game fish. The herrings are all schooling fishes that can be readily identified by their silvery sides, single dorsal fin, soft-rayed fins, and their lack of an adipose fin.

AMERICAN SHAD (Alosa sapidissima) (Figure 4)

Alias: Shad.

Habitat: Little is known about the marine distribution of shad off the Washington coast.

Lures: Rarely taken by anglers in the marine environment. Caught in fresh water on a variety of very small, bright and metallic-colored lures.

Table value: Good, if properly prepared or canned. Shad roe is generally considered a delicacy.

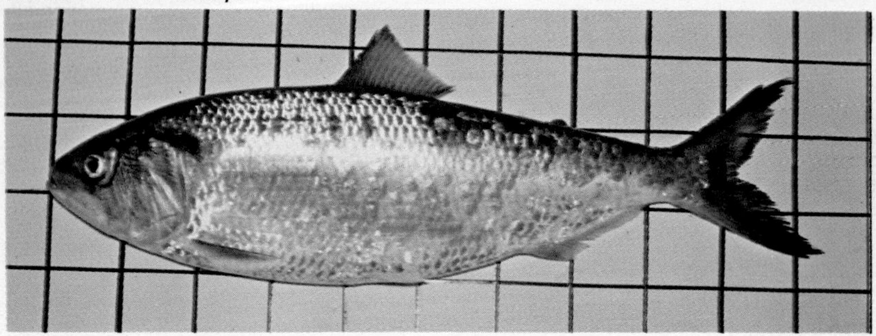

Figure 4, American Shad

Shad spawn in rivers, the females depositing small eggs that drift with the current. Shad are the only abundant local marine fish that are not native to Washington. Our shad resulted from introductions into the Sacramento and Columbia Rivers in 1871 from the East Coast. The Columbia River hosts a large shad run and smaller runs occur in the Chehalis and Willapa Rivers. Shad ascend the Columbia River in late spring, but the best angling is in June and July. The only significant sport fisheries in Washington occur at the mouth of the Washougal River (Camas Slough) and from the bank immediately below Bonneville Dam. The average weight of adult Columbia River shad is about 3 1/2 pounds and the maximum is about 8 pounds. However, shad to 13 1/2 pounds have been recorded elsewhere. Shad are splendid sport fish and when hooked, appear to be about as strong and fast as trout and salmon.

PACIFIC HERRING (Clupea pallasii) (Figure 5 Bottom)

Alias: Herring

Habitat: Seasonally abundant throughout Puget Sound, Juan de Fuca Strait and in coastal areas. Spawning typically occurs during the winter and early spring in shallow water. The adhesive eggs are spawned onto eel grass and other seaweeds where they may be exposed at low tide.

Lures: Taken on bare hooks by jigging.

Table value: Excellent when pickled.

Herring are very familiar to anglers as the principal bait for salmon and other marine fishes. A useful method for collecting herring, however, is by "jigging" which could be considered a form of angling. Large (8-12 inch) herring doubtlessly could be taken on small flies cast into schools feeding on the surface. The maximum length of Pacific herring is reported to be 13 inches.

SMELT FAMILY (Osmeridae) (Figure 5 Top)

Smelt are small unspotted, silvery fishes with only soft-rayed fins and an adipose fin. Although several species of smelt occur in our waters, only the surf smelt is taken in saltwater on hook and line.

SURF SMELT (Hypomesus pretiosus)

Alias: Silver smelt

Habitat: Little is known about the offshore distribution of surf smelt. They regularly occur in certain areas and spawn on specific gravel beaches.

Lures: Usually taken by "jigging".

Table value: Excellent – usually fried.

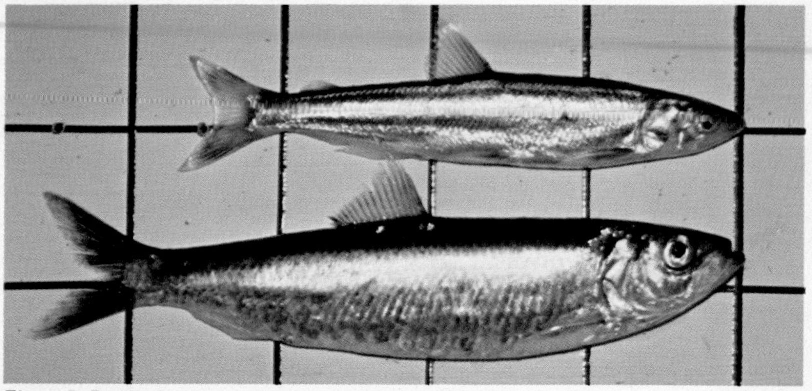

Figure 5, Pacific Herring (bottom) and Surf Smelt (top)

Smelt are taken by jigging from piers and floats principally during late winter. This type of fishing is very popular in Swinomish Slough at LaConner where an annual smelt derby is held. They are also jigged at Everett, in the vicinity of Bellingham, and in recent years, at the mouth of Woodard Creek near Olympia. The average length of surf smelt is about 8 inches and the maximum about 10 inches.

Smelt dipping, with special nets, is popular during the summer months at certain beaches on the coast, strait and sound – notably at Kalaloch, Twin Rivers and Utsaladdy, Camano Island respectively. The smelt are dipped as they come into the very shallow water to spawn during an approximately two-hour period before and after high tide.

salmon **salmon**

SALMON FAMILY (Salmonidae)

This is the most well known group of fishes to local anglers. All five North American species of Pacific salmon are abundant in our marine waters and spawn in Washington streams. A sixth species of Pacific salmon, the masu salmon (Oncorhynchus masu), occurs along the Asiatic coast of the North Pacific with the five other species. All of Washington's native trout and char also occur in salt water as well as in fresh water.

The members of the salmon family occurring in saltwater all spawn in freshwater. Typically, these fish return to their natal streams and spawn in a nest dug in clean gravel by the female. Pacific salmon and Dolly Varden are fall spawners while steelhead and cutthroat are classed as spring spawners. Pacific salmon die after spawning, but trout (Salmo sp.) and char (Salvelinus sp.) may not.

The predominant salt-water colors of members of the salmon family are silvery sides, a white underside, and a dark, usually spotted, back. The fins of these fishes are supported only by soft rays and they all have an adipose fin. The smelts, which are closely related to salmon and trout, also have an adipose fin but smelt are unspotted small fishes that are taken by "jigging" and netting rather than by normal angling.

Pacific Salmon can be separated from trout by counting the soft rays in the anal fin. A count of the unbranched bases of the anal fin rays will be less than 12 for trout and char and 12 or more for Pacific salmon. In addition, the tail fins of trout appear more "square" and catchable sized salmon have dark pigment inside their mouths but the insides of the mouths of the trout are essentially white. Dolly Varden are the only local marine salmonids with light colored spots on their backs and sides.

CHINOOK SALMON (Oncorhynchus tshawytscha) (Figure 6)

Aliases: King, blackmouth, spring, tyee

Habitat: See page 90.

Baits and lures: See page 54.

Table value: Excellent.

Figure 6, Chinook Salmon

Chinook salmon are the largest of the six species of Pacific salmon. A giant of 126 pounds, caught commercially in Alaska, is the largest on record and a 92-pounder from the Skeena River, British Columbia, is the largest sport-caught fish. The Washington sport record is a 70 1/2 pounder from Juan de Fuca Strait in 1964.

Chinook spawn in our large unspoiled streams from late summer to late fall. The time of upstream spawning migration varies with the race of fish and extends from February through October in Washington. Typically, the large glacial or colder river systems host spring runs of chinook and in the longer river systems these fish typically utilize the head waters for spawning. Later "running" fish typically spawn nearer the sea. Although there are some remarkable exceptions, male chinook usually mature at ages 2 to 5 while females mature at age 4 or 5. The young of late run or "fall chinook" usually migrate to sea during the first spring of life, while the young of early running fish or "spring chinook" usually spend a year in fresh water before migrating to sea. Most of the fish weighing 40 pounds or more taken in Washington appear to be in at least their fifth year of life. The largest race of Washington chinook may well be the Skagit River summer run, but very large fish also return to the Quillayute, Hoh, Queets, Quinault, and Humptulips Rivers.

Mature 2-year-old male chinook are called "jacks". Chinook showing no signs of sexual maturity are locally called "blackmouth" while larger fish, or those showing signs of sexual maturity, are called "kings". As chinook salmon approach sexual maturity, their scales become more firmly imbedded and their predominant color changes from silver to various shades of brown. As with all Pacific salmon, the maturing male develops a hook snout, large canine teeth, and "razor- back".

The runs of chinook salmon in Washington have been greatly enhanced by artificial production and, due to the continuing losses of our natural fresh water environment, the future of chinook angling in Washington doubtlessly depends on continuing and accelerated hatchery programs.

COHO SALMON (Oncorhynchus kisutch) (Figure 7)

Aliases: Silver, hooknose.

Habitat: See page 90.

Baits and lures: See page 54.

Table value: Excellent.

Figure 7, Coho Salmon

In terms of numbers of salmon caught in recent years, coho have comprised about 60 per cent of the Washington salmon sport catch. Washington coho salmon usually mature at 3 years of age, although sexually precocious 2-year-old males ("jacks") are common in hatchery runs. Coho salmon spawn in virtually all of our small, unspoiled lowland streams. Adult coho typically enter their natal streams with the October freshets and spawn in November and December; however, there are some notable exceptions. Most Columbia River coho enter the main stem in early September and spawn the following month. Young coho typically spend a full year in fresh water, migrating to sea during the spring of their second year of life. Since these young coho rear in the small er streams, the ultimate survival of wild coho depends upon adequate stream flows during this early fresh-water existence. Since the coho fishing at any one time is dependent on a single age group of fish, a dry summer can damage coho fishing for an entire season as occurred in the disastrous year of 1960 when the fishing was ruined by the summer drought of 1958. Conversely, 1970 was a record coho run as was the western Washington summer rainfall of 1968.

The local coho population has been greatly supplemented by artificial hatchery production in recent years. Nowhere is this more evident than in the booming sport fishery at the mouth of the Columbia River.

The record coho is a 31-pound fish taken by an angler at Cowichan Bay, Vancouver Island, B.C.. The largest Washington sport-caught coho recorded is a 26 pound fish taken at Westport, Washington. Nearly all of the catches of big "silvers" (more than 20 pounds) that biologists are asked to verify are actually chinook salmon lacking tail spotting, but these fish always possess the black lower gumline. The largest "race" of Washington coho (20 pounders are not uncommon) appears to be those entering the Chehalis River system in late November and December. Anglers, however, have been slow to exploit these big fish. The spawning colors of coho salmon are reddish sides with dark backs.

PINK SALMON (Oncorhynchus gorbuscha) (Figure 8)

Aliases: Humpback salmon, humpie.

Habitat: See page 90.

Baits and lures: See page 54.

Table value: Excellent.

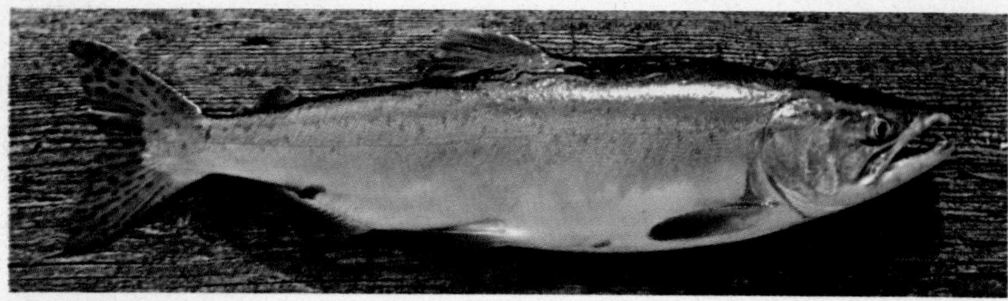

Figure 8, Pink Salmon

The large, cold river systems of (Nisqually, Puyallup) Puget Sound are essentially the southern extremity of the pink salmon's North American spawning range. However, a few occasionally appear in streams as far south as the Sacramento River, California. Spawning pink salmon are 2 year olds. Many streams in northern British Columbia and Alaska have even year runs. Local pink salmon typically spawn in October and the young leave the stream during the early spring of the following year soon after emerging from spawning gravel. The spawning colors of pink salmon are brownish above with white on lower sides and belly. The maximum weight for this species appears to be about 15 pounds with large fish most evident in years of poor abundance.

CHUM SALMON (Oncorhynchus keta) (Figure 9)

Aliases: Dog salmon, fall salmon

Habitat: Adult chum salmon apparently move quickly through our coastal waters from their feeding areas in the North Pacific. Fry and fingerlings of locally spawned chum are abundant in Puget Sound during the spring.

Baits and lures: Occasionally taken by salmon anglers on herring and herring-strip baits.

Table value: Excellent – especially when smoked or kippered.

In recent years, up to two thousand chum salmon have been taken annually by Washington marine anglers. They are rather common in fall sport catches at Point No Point, Hood Canal, southern Puget Sound, and in the Chehalis River. Large hook-and-line catches (floating set lines) have been made in North Pacific by the Japanese using salted anchovies for bait. Up until the 1940's, there was a specific sport fishery for chum at Gig Harbor, near Tacoma. These anglers primarily used herring-strip baits. Chum salmon populations have undergone a serious decline throughout the southern portion of their North American range.

Typically, chum spawn in the late fall rather close to salt water. Soon after

Figure 9, Chum Salmon

emerging from the gravel, the young migrate to sea. Local runs are comprised primarily of three, four, and five-year- old fish. The spawning colors of chum salmon are predominantly olive with streaks of red and yellow. The maximum weight of chum salmon is about 33 pounds.

SOCKEYE SALMON (Oncorhynchus nerka) (Figure 10)

Aliases: Red salmon (Alaska), blue back (Columbia and Quinault Rivers). Kokanee or "silver trout" are names used for the land-locked form.

Habitat: Like chum salmon, adult sockeye apparently move quickly through our coastal waters from their feeding areas in the North Pacific.

Table value: Excellent – most of the catch is canned.

Figure 10, Sockeye Salmon

Although millions of these salmon migrate through our marine waters annually, only a few hundred are taken by anglers. However, as with chum salmon, Japanese floating set lines have taken large numbers of sockeye in the North Pacific. Canadian commercial trollers have also begun to catch sockeye off the west coast of Vancouver Island using flashers and small plastic squid-like lures. In Alaska, sea-run sockeye are important sport fish in streams where they are taken on various artificial lures.

Sockeye typically spawn in tributaries to lakes but they also utilize certain gravelly beaches in the lakes. The young usually spend a year rearing in a lake before migrating to sea. In Washington, sockeye occur in the Columbia, Quinault, Ozette, Skagit, and Lake Washington systems. Local sea-run sockeye mature primarily in from 3 to 5 years. Their maximum weight is about 15 pounds. The spawning colors of sockeye are red on back and sides and a greenish head.

Landlocked sockeye salmon (kokanee) are very important to local anglers and are stocked in many lakes in and outside of their natural range. These fish spend their entire lives within a lake system area. Like other Pacific salmon, kokanee die after spawning.

STEELHEAD (RAINBOW) TROUT (Salmo gairdneri) (Figure 11)

Aliases: Steelhead – a sea-run rainbow trout. The term rainbow trout is used for fresh water forms.

Habitat: Steelhead apparently spend most of their marine lives well offshore in the North Pacific. They appear to be on spawning and post-spawning migrations when taken by marine anglers.

Lures: Most steelhead taken from salt-water are caught on artificial spoons and "bobbers". In addition, a few are taken incidentally on various types of salmon lures.

Table value: Excellent.

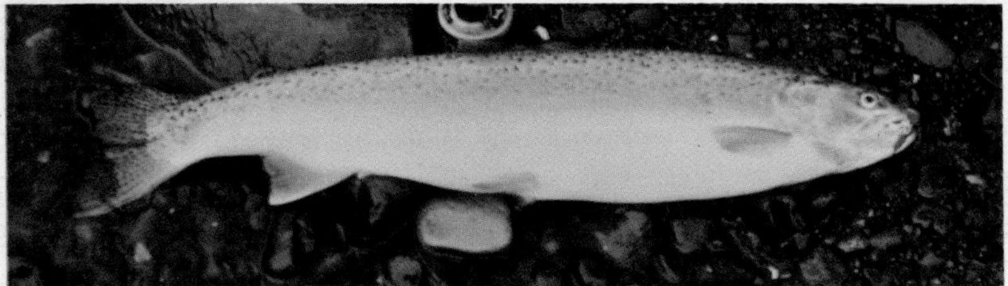

Figure 11, Steelhead Trout **Stan Jones Photo**

Relatively few steelhead are taken by salt water anglers fishing in specific locations – notably during the winter months on the beaches at Bush and Lagoon Points, Whidbey Island. In addition, they are occasionally taken incidentally by salmon anglers, but many of these fish are spawned-out (kelt) fish taken during the spring.

Steelhead typically first mature in their third, fourth, or fifth year of life. The young fish spend two or three years in the stream before migrating to sea. However, hatchery-reared steelhead are released at migratory size after one year in fresh water and these fish return predominantly as 3-year-olds. Although steelhead trout are capable of spawning more than once, they apparently suffer high post-spawning mortalities and returns are predominantly comprised of initial spawners.

The Washington sport catch is primarily dependent upon fish entering the streams during the winter months but some rivers, notably the Columbia system, also contain larger numbers of summer and spring-run fish. These fish, as well as winter run steelhead, spawn during the late winter- early spring period. Like spring chinook, they store considerable amounts of body fats for sustenance in fresh water.

The world record steelhead trout is a 42-pounder from Southeast Alaska. The Washington record is a 33-pound steelhead from the Snake River.

CUTTHROAT TROUT (Salmo clarki) (Figure 12)

Aliases: Sea-run cutthroat, sea-run, cutthroat, harvest trout, "blueback".

Habitat: Occurs in virtually all of our large and small unspoiled coastal streams. Sea-run forms are present within the inter-tidal zones (between the low and high tide marks) in most of our marine areas.

Baits and lures: Spoons, spinners, small cut bait from herring, sandlance, and sculpin bellies, salmon roe.

Table value: Good.

Figure 12, Cutthroat Trout

Cutthroat trout exhibit remarkable variation, principally in color and spotting, throughout their natural range so that it is far easier to distinguish Yellowstone cutthroat from coastal cutthroat than it is coastal cutthroat from rainbow (steelhead) trout. Coastal cutthroat often lack the red "cutthroat marks" on either side of the lower jaw. Mature "sea-runs" usually range between 10 and 20 inches in length – anything larger is an exceptional fish. The largest specimens are from lakes. A cutthroat weighing over 40 pounds was once taken from Pyramid Lake, Nevada. The Washington State record cutthroat is 8 3/4 lbs. from an eastern Washington lake. The maximum size for "sea-runs" is about 5 lbs.

Cutthroat trout are late winter-early spring spawners, although "sea-runs" typically ascend rivers from late summer through fall. Puget Sound cutthroat tend to move into streams later than Juan de Fuca Strait and ocean cutthroat. Most salt-water-caught cutthroat are taken within the inter-tidal zone.

DOLLY VARDEN (Salvelinus malma) (Figure 13)

Aliases: Dolly Varden trout, Dolly, bull trout.

Habitat: Typically occur in colder river systems (of glacial origin) and associated deep lakes. Sea-run fish occur in and near the estuaries of Dolly Varden streams, frequently in the inter-tidal zone.

Bait and lures: A good "spoon" and plug fish but also taken on salmon roe in both fresh and salt water.

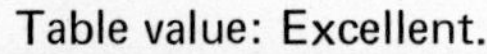

Table value: Excellent.

Figure 13, Dolly Varden

The Dolly Varden is the only member of the salmon family found in salt water that has light colored spots on its back and sides. All other members of the family have dark colored spots. Sea-run Dolly Varden typically ascend local streams in mid-summer and spawn in the streams in the fall. Mature sea-run fish usually range from 15-25 inches in length. (The specimen pictured, a male, is exceptionally large for a sea-run fish.) Lake and reservoir-reared fish attain the largest size, with the record being a 32-pound specimen from Lake Pend Oreille, Idaho. The Washington State record is a 22 1/2 pounder. The best salt-water fishing for these fish apparently occurs during the spring in and adjacent to the Skagit River estuaries and at certain locations in Saratoga Passage and Port Susan. Most of the marine-caught Dollies are taken within the inter-tidal zone.

CODFISH AND HAKE FAMILY (Gadidae)

Members of this family are elongated, round-bodied fishes usually having three dorsal and two anal fins. The fins of these fishes lack spines. Although the Pacific hake is included in this family, its second dorsal fin and single anal fin are only deeply "notched", but hake appear to have the standard codfish fin counts. Some scientists include hake in a different but closely related family (Merlucciidae). The burbot ("fresh-water lingcod"), the only fresh-water member of the cod family, occurs in certain Washington lakes in the upper Columbia River system. This same fish is also found in certain lakes in Europe, northern Asia, and else where in northern North America. The burbot is closely related to the European ling (Molva sp.) rather than to salt-water lingcod (Ophiodon elongatus).

PACIFIC COD (Gadus macrocephalus) (Figure 14, Middle)

Aliases: Cod, true cod.

Habitat: A schooling, moving fish usually found near a smooth, firm bottom in more than 80 feet of water. It is especially abundant from winter through early spring in northern Puget Sound, but is locally abundant as far south as Anderson Island in Puget Sound.

Bait and lures: Herring, metal jigs.

Table value: Excellent, usually filleted and fried.

Pacific cod, like many of our other deep-water fish, are dull when hooked, but they are fine food fish. Most skilled cod anglers take them on plain metal jigs. The cod attain weights of more than 20 lbs. in local waters and have been taken over 40 pounds in Alaska. Pacific cod can be distinguished from walleye pollock in that the former possesses a prominent barbel (whisker) and an upper jaw that extends beyond the lower jaw.

PACIFIC TOMCOD (Microgadus proximus) (Figure 14, Top)

Aliases: Tomcod, (small) cod.

Habitat: A migrating schooling fish, abundant during the summer months in coastal harbors and bays and seasonally abundant in Puget Sound. They are often taken around piers and floats.

Bait: Indiscriminate feeders.

Table value: Good, although too small to fillet.

Tomcod are too small to interest most anglers, but they do provide good sport for youngsters. The maximum length is about 12 inches. Pacific tomcod can be distinguished from small Pacific cod in that the latter has a larger barbel (whisker) and its anus is directly under its second, rather than its first, dorsal fin.

WALLEYE POLLOCK (Theragra chalcogrammus) (Figure 14, Bottom)

Aliases: Cod, popeye.

Habitat: A moving, schooling fish usually found near bottom in depths over 75 feet. Seasonally abundant in many areas in Puget Sound and Juan de Fuca Strait.

Bait: Herring

Table value: Fair, although quite soft and often heavily parasitized.

These fish have little to offer anglers. They are seldom available to youngsters on piers and are most often discarded when caught by boat fishermen. The maximum length is about three feet.

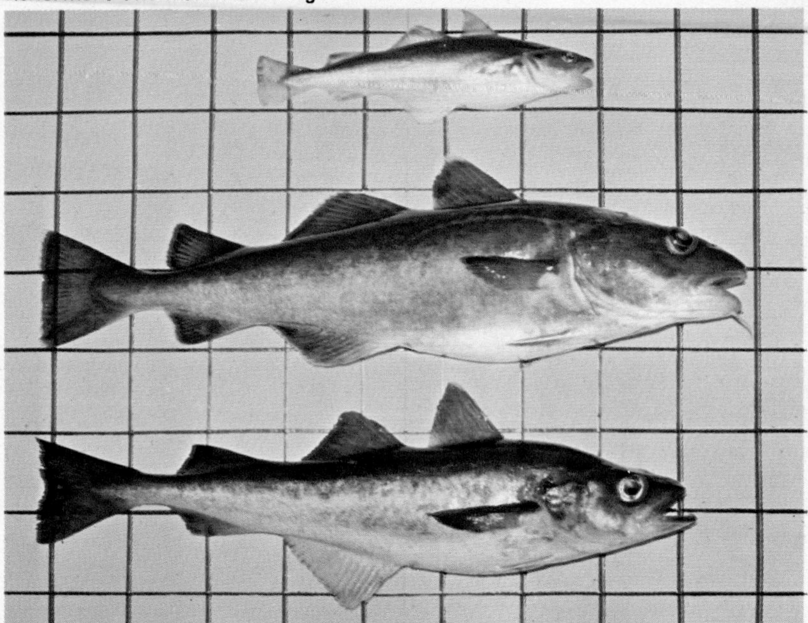

Figure 14, Pacific Cod (middle), Pacific Tomcod (top), Walleye Pollock (bottom)

These fish have little to offer anglers. They are seldom available to youngsters on piers and are most often discarded when caught by boat fishermen. The maximum length is about three feet.

PACIFIC HAKE (Merluccius productus) (Figure 15)

Alias: Hake.

Habitat: A schooling, moving fish usually found over a smooth bottom in water deeper than 150 feet. Pacific hake may be abundant just off bottom or on the surface – the latter situation frequently occurs at night.

Bait: Herring.

Table value: Good, although they will become soft if not cleaned and cooled quickly.

Figure 15, Pacific Hake

From an angler's viewpoint, the most exciting thing about hake is that they leave a salmon-like bite mark on a herring bait. In recent years, Pacific hake have been exploited heavily off the Washington coast primarily by Russian trawlers. The Russians process these fish quickly and freeze them for later human consumption. The Pacific hake taken by American fishermen are primarily reduced for animal food. In late winter and early spring hake are concentrated in Port Susan, Puget Sound, where they are heavily exploited by local trawlers. This group of fish is apparently part of a population that remains in Puget Sound. The maximum length of hake is reported to be three feet, but it appears to be much smaller locally.

SURFPERCH FAMILY (Embiotocidae)

The surfperches are rather small, flat-sided fishes with fins supported by both sharp spines and soft rays. Their pectoral fins are long, delicate and semi-transparent. Although many other fishes bear live young, this family is remarkable in that prior to birth the young are nourished through a placental-type structure rather than with nutrients contained within the egg. The surfperches are fine sport fish.

REDTAIL SURFPERCH (Amphistichus rhodoterus) (Figure 16, Bottom)

Aliases: Seaperch, perch, redtails.

Habitat: Abundant in the surf along ocean beaches and on Juan de Fuca Strait beaches as far east as Twin Rivers.

Baits and lures: Razor clam parts, mussels, shrimp, ghost shrimp, shore crabs, small polychaete worms, small spoons.

Table value: Good. Difficult to fillet – best cleaned and fried with skin on. Bones and skin are easily removed after cooking.

Figure 16, Redtail Surfperch (bottom), Striped Seaperch (top)

This is the ocean beach surf fish in Washington. They are attractive, scrappy, and will take a variety of natural baits as well as small wobbling spoons. Redtails are not exploited by local commercial fishermen and are very abundant in some areas. Robert Mausolf, a fisheries instructor at Peninsula College at Port Angeles, reported catching and releasing over 6,000 redtails in a single set of a 150 foot beach seine at Twin Rivers Juan de Fuca Strait in 1967. The maximum length of these fish is about 16 inches.

STRIPED SEAPERCH (Embiotoca lateralis) (Figure 16, Top)

Aliases: Blue perch, perch

Habitat: Occurs in shallow waters during the late spring through early winter months throughout Puget Sound, Juan de Fuca Strait and in protected bays along the outer coast. Apparently retreats to deeper waters during the late winter through early spring months. Prefers areas with profuse growths of barnacles and mussels as well as eelgrass beds.

Baits: Polychaetous worms, shrimp, ghost shrimp, mussels, and shore crabs.

Table value: Same as redtail surfperch.

One of the most attractive local fishes. Often visible grazing among pier pilings with heavy cultures of mussels and barnacles. A fine little fish with surprising speed and strength. Striped seaperch are selective feeders, often rejecting a baited hook after close examination. They are best taken on a light leader, light sinker and a small hook (a size No. 4 is recommended). Striped seaperch and pileperch can sometimes by "chumed" (attracted into biting) by scraping barnacles and mussels loose from a piling. The maximum length is about 15 inches.

PILE PERCH (Rhacochilus vacca) (Figure 17)

Aliases: Silver perch, perch

Habitat: Similar to the striped seaperch, however, it apparently is more of a moving, schooling fish and is often abundant in the inter-tidal zone at the heads of mud-bottomed bays.

Bait: Same as for striped seaperch.

Table value: Similar to redtail surfperch.

Figure 17, Pile Perch

The pile perch is as fine a sport fish as the striped seaperch and it grows to a larger size. Maximum length about 17 inches.

SHINER PERCH (Cymatogaster aggregata) (Figure 18)

Aliases: Yellow shiner, shiner, pogy.

Habitat: A schooling, moving fish, abundant from late spring through late fall in shallow waters. Apparently moves into deeper water in winter. Frequently observed in tight schools over shallow water, feeding on the surface.

Bait: Very indiscriminate.

Table value: Dried and pickled extensively by Oriental Americans.

Figure 18, Shiner Perch

Shiner perch are too small to interest most anglers. A small bait and hook (a No. 12 is recommended) is necessary to take them. They are a fine live bait for rockfish and occasionally are eaten by salmon. Schools of three- to seven-inch fish observed "sculling" about with their pectoral fins are usually shiner perch. Maximum length about eight inches.

ROCKFISH FAMILY (Scorpaenidae)

Rockfish are heavy-boned, spiny fishes, large through the head and "shoulders". Although they are bass-like in appearance, based on internal characteristics they are in a family separate from sea bass (Serranidae) and fresh-water "bass" (Micropterus sp.). The term "cod" is even more inappropriate for the rockfishes.

COPPER ROCKFISH (Sebastodes caurinus) (Figure 19)

Alias: "Rockcod".

Habitat: Prefers rocky bottom areas but is widely distributed in Puget Sound and Juan de Fuca Strait. Often found in shallow water around rocks, kelp, or pilings during the summer but most frequently taken from depths greater than 50 feet.

Baits and lures: Herring, shiner perch (best live), shrimp, large polychaete worms, jigs.

Table value: Excellent, usually filleted and fried.

Figure 19, Copper Rockfish

This is the most important rockfish to Puget Sound anglers. Can be quite scrappy on light gear in shallow water but is unimpressive when taken from depths. WCSDC record ten pounds.

QUILLBACK ROCKFISH (Sebastodes maliger) (Figure 20)

Alias: "Rockcod"

Habitat: Usually restricted to rocky bottoms below 50 feet. Can be very abundant on rocky reefs in areas of strong tidal current. Common in Puget Sound, especially in northern areas, and in Juan de Fuca Strait.

Baits and lures: Same as for copper rockfish.

Table value: Excellent tasting fish, usually filleted and fried.

Figure 20, Quillback Rockfish

One of the most common rockfishes in sport catches. Most fishermen do not distinguish quillback from the copper rockfish, however, the former can be identified by the orange-brown (rust colored) spots of the "throat" area.

BLUE ROCKFISH (Sebastodes mystinus) (Figure 21, Top)

Aliases: "Bass", "seabass", "black seabass".

Habitat: Similar to the black rockfish. Uncommon inside of Cape Flattery, but abundant along the northwestern side of the Olympic Peninsula.

Baits and lures: Similar to black rockfish.

Table value: Good.

Only the angler-naturalist is likely to distinguish blue from black rockfish. In the blue, the upper jaw or maxillary extends only to the middle of the eye when the mouth is closed and in the black rockfish, it extends at least to the rear edge of the eye. In addition, when the anal fin is extended on the black rockfish, its upper rear corner is in front of the lower rear corner of the fin, while in the blue, either the reverse is true or the corners are vertically in line. The blue rockfish is a very important sport fish along the central California coast. Maximum length is 21 inches.

BLACK ROCKFISH (Sebastodes melanops) (Figure 21, Bottom)

Aliases: "bass", "seabass", "black seabass"

Habitat: Abundant during summer in shallow water along the rocky kelp-lined shores of the outer coast, Juan de Fuca Strait, and the San Juan Islands, but is more restricted in distribution on inner Puget Sound. Apparently retreats to deeper water during late fall through early spring months.

Baits and lures: Jigs, herring, and even surface plugs and flies when fish are showing on the surface.

Table value: Good, usually filleted and fried.

Figure 21, Blue Rockfish (top), Black Rockfish (bottom)

This rockfish is a fine sport fish when taken from shallow water. Large schools of black rockfish feeding on the surface are a common sight along the shores of western Juan de Fuca Strait. When fishing close to shore, it is not uncommon to observe one of these fish pass by a herring bait to grab the sinker. Black rockfish prefer a moving or spinning bait or lure. These fish are apparently attracted to light and can be taken readily at night on feathered jigs. The black rockfish is the most common rockfish in the Washington sport catch. WCSDC record 10 pounds, 6 ounces.

CANARY ROCKFISH (Sebastodes pinniger) (Figure 22)

Figure 22, Canary Rockfish

Alias: "Red snapper".

Habitat: Always taken near bottom and usually in depths over 150 feet. These fish are not restricted to rocky bottom areas. They occur in certain locations as far south as Point Defiance, Puget Sound and are more abundant among the San Juan Islands, northern Puget Sound and Juan de Fuca Strait.

Bait and lures: Herring, large jigs.

Table value: Excellent, usually filleted and fried.

Canary rockfish are apparently deep water schooling fish associated with specific bottom locations. Since they are most often located well away from land, it is usually necessary to triangulate one's position to locate a productive area. Once this is done, fishing for these fish can be most productive. The WCSDC record is 9 lb. 10 oz.

RASPHEAD ROCKFISH (Sebastodes ruberrimus) (Figure 23)

Alias: "Red snapper"

Habitat: Always found near bottom, usually in depths greater than 150 feet over rocks. Occurs in northern Puget Sound, Juan de Fuca Strait, and along the outer coast.

Bait: Herring.

Table value: Excellent, usually filleted and fried.

Figure 23, Rasphead Rockfish

Few anglers distinguish this red rockfish from the canary rockfish (both are usually called "red snapper"), but the rasphead can be distinguished by the black edges on its soft-rayed fins. There are no members of the snapper family (Lutjanidae) off Washington's coast although rasphead and canary rockfish are marketed as "red snapper". This is one of the largest of our rockfish. The WCSDC record is 23 pounds.

CHINA ROCKFISH (Sebastodes nebulosus) (Figure 24)

Aliases: "Bass", "rockcod".

Habitat: Common during the summer months along the steep shorelines of western Juan de Fuca Strait and the outer coast.

Baits and lures: Herring, jigs.

Table value: Excellent, usually filleted and fried.

China rockfish appear to inhabit the depths just below those occupied by black rockfish. They are unimpressive when hooked. The WCSDC record is 3 pounds, 7 ounces.

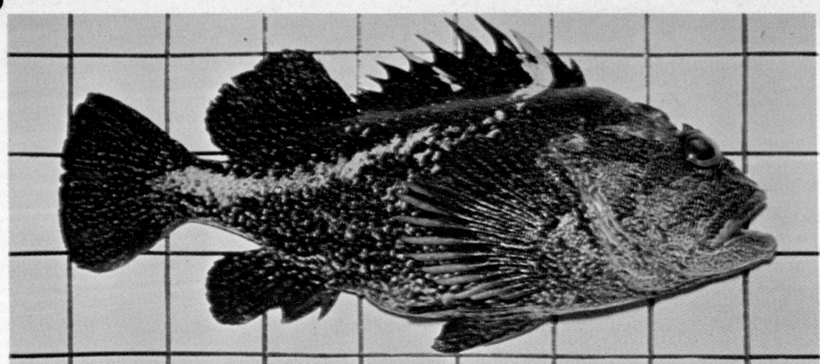

Figure 24, China Rockfish

YELLOWTAIL ROCKFISH (Sebastodes flavidus) (Figure 25)

Alias: "Bass".

Habitat: Schools of yellowtail rockfish are encountered sporadically in Puget Sound. They occur more commonly in the ocean catches from offshore waters where they appear either on the bottom or near the surface.

Bait and lures: Herring, jigs.

Table value: Excellent, usually filleted and fried.

Figure 25, Yellowtail Rockfish

When near the surface, yellowtail rockfish are frequently caught by salmon fisherman. Duncan and Duntz rocks, at the entrance to Juan de Fuca Strait, usually harbor large and hungry schools of yellowtail rockfish. They are strong fish when hooked in shallow water. The WCSDC record is 6 pounds, 6 ounces.

WIDOW ROCKFISH (Sebastodes entomelas) (Figure 26)

Figure 26, Widow Rockfish

Aliases: "Bass", "brown bomber".

Habitat: Common in sport catches off the southwest Washington coast but infrequently taken by state anglers elsewhere.

Baits and lures: Herring, jigs.

Table value: Excellent, usually filleted and fried.

This is another of the rockfishes that is quite game when hooked.

SABLEFISH FAMILY (Anoplopomatidae)

The sablefishes are elongated, round bodied, smooth-headed and have two dorsal fins. Their fin spines are not prickly. There are only two members of the family and one, the skilfish, is rare.

SABLEFISH (Anoplopoma fimbria) (Figure 27)

Aliases: "Blackcod", "mackerel".

Habitat: Often abundant in open waters near the surface in and around the tide rips from the Tacoma Narrows through northern Puget Sound, especially near the southern tip of Whidbey Island.

Baits: Herring.

Table value: The flesh has a high oil content that results in an excellent smoked product.

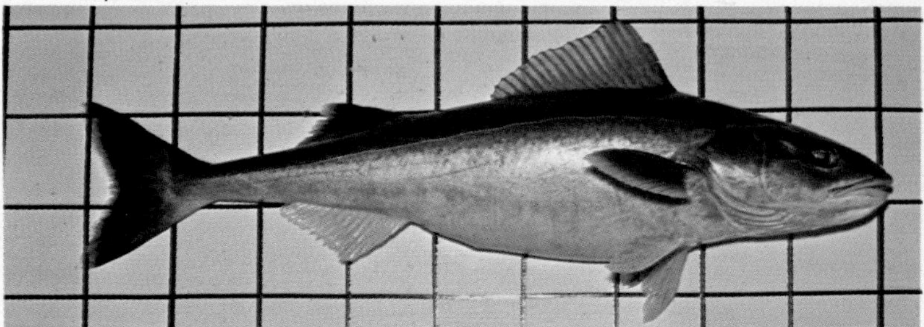

Figure 27, Sablefish

Most sport-caught sablefish are caught incidentally by salmon anglers trolling or "mooching" with herring bait. They appear to be only young sablefish since they are typically small, uniform in size, and grow noticeably from winter through early fall. Although sablefish reach weights of 40 pounds, a two pounder is a good size for Puget Sound. Large fish from the North Pacific have been taken from depths as great as 1,000 feet. Literature indicates a slow growth rate for sablefish, but specimens taken from Puget Sound and exhibited in the Point Defiance aquarium, Tacoma, have grown at a remarkable rate.

SCULPIN FAMILY (Cottidae)

Many species of sculpins occur in local marine and fresh waters, but most are small and are seldom seen by anglers. Members of the family typically have large, flattened, horny heads having given rise to the name "bullhead". These fish, however, should not be confused with members of the fresh-water catfish family (Ictaluridae) which possess barbels ("whiskers") and an adipose fin. Sculpins have very large pectoral fins and when out of water, their body shape is such that they rest on their bellies rather than on their sides.

PACIFIC STAGHORN SCULPIN (Leptocottus armatus) (Figure 28)

Alias: Bullhead.

Habitat: Sandy and mixed sand and rock bottoms found within and just below the inter-tidal zone. Apparently avoids surf.

Baits and lures: A greedy and indiscriminate feeder. Will frequently chase an artificial lure to the surface in shallow water.

Table value: Good. Remove the head and viscera, clean and fry.

Figure 28, Pacific Staghorn Sculpin

Staghorn sculpins are common in shallow water throughout Puget Sound where they will bury themselves in sand for cover. They have provided a great deal of recreation for youngsters and are taken in large numbers from piers and shore. The maximum length is about 12 inches.

BUFFALO SCULPIN (Enophrys bison) (Figure 29)

Alias: Bullhead.

Habitat: Similar to the Red Irish Lord, but appears to prefer shallower water and an abundance of seaweed.

Baits: Herring, crabs, mussels, polychaete worms.

Table value: Probably good, but a rather small tidbit.

Figure 29, Buffalo Sculpin

The fish are commonly taken by youngsters and are usually discarded. Their large "horns" are a remarkable characteristic.

RED IRISH LORD (Hemilepidotus hemilepidotus) (Figure 30)

Alias: Bullhead.

Habitat: Occurs on the bottom near rocks, rubble or pilings below and in the lower inter-tidal zone. Individuals from deeper water are reddish in color while those taken from shallow water are predominantly brown.

Baits: Herring, crab, mussels, polychaete worms.

Table value: Apparently good.

These fish are only occasionally taken by anglers. Maximum length is about 12 inches.

See next page.

Figure 30, Red Irish Lord See previous page.

CABEZON (Scorpaenichthys marmoratus) (Figure 31)

Aliases: "Bullcod", bullhead, giant marbled sculpin.

Habitat: Occurs below and in the lower inter-tidal zone, usually on rock and sand bottoms.

Baits: Crab, live shiner perch, and live herring.

Table value: Good, usually filleted and fried. Like the lingcod, the flesh may be blue-green, but will turn white when cooked.

Warning: Cabezon roe (eggs) are reported to be poisonous.

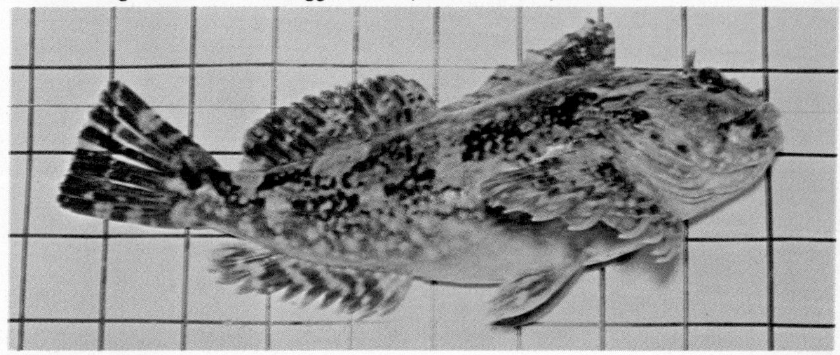

Figure 31, Cabezon

Cabezon are the most important fish, by weight, in the Washington skin diving harvest. Relatively few are taken by anglers indicating that ordinary herring bait is ineffective for cabezon. The sight of a large cabezon in shallow water dashing for cover in a "cloud" of sand is always exciting. The WCSDC record is 22 pounds, 4 ounces.

GREENLING FAMILY (Hexagramidae)

The greenlings are elongated, round-bodied, often colorful fishes with no boney projections or spines on their heads. They appear to have two dorsal fins, but actually it is a single, deeply-notched fin. They have long anal fins and pectoral fins that are large and rounded.

LINGCOD (Ophiodon elongatus) (Figure 32)

Alias: "Ling".

Habitat: Frequents the depths below the inter-tidal zone among boulders, rubble, and reefs, usually in areas of strong tidal currents.

Baits and lures: Herring (best live), live greenling, flounder, rockfish, large jigs, octopus.

Table value: Excellent, usually filleted or steaked and fried. Some lingcod have blue-green bodies and flesh, but this is harmless and the flesh turns white when cooked.

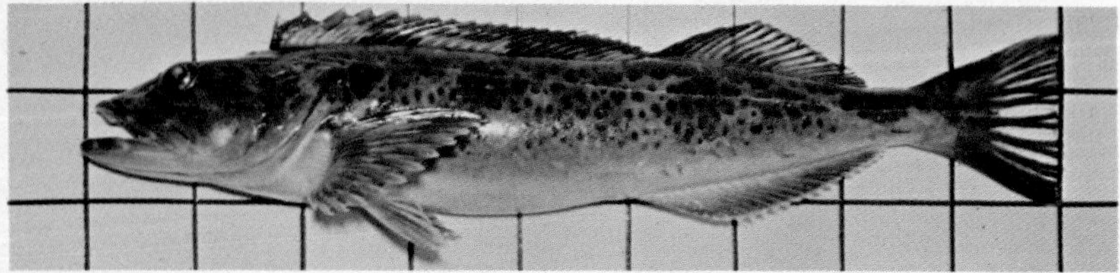
Figure 32, Lingcod

Although not spectacular when hooked, the powerful rushes of lingcod for freedom through kelp and among encrusted boulders are often successful. Lingcod teeth abrade nylon. The WCSDC record is 82 pounds, 1 ounce.

KELP GREENLING (Hexagrammos decagrammus) (Figures 33, 34)

Aliases: "kelpcod", "rocktrout"

Habitat: Rocky, kelp-lined shorelines and reefs below the inter-tidal zone. Especially abundant among the San Juan Islands, Juan de Fuca Strait, and along the northern Washington coast.

Baits and lures: Herring, polychaete worms, small jigs, shrimp.

Table value: Excellent, usually filleted and fried.

Figure 33, Male Kelp Greenling

Figure 34, Female Kelp Greenling

Kelp greenling are one of the gamier and handsome bottomfish. As noted elsewhere, they are fine bait for lingcod. The WCSDC record is 4 pounds, 10 ounces. The photographs indicate the varying color phases and the interesting difference between male and female.

WHITESPOTTED GREENLING (Hexagrammos stelleri) (Figure 35)

Aliases: "Kelpcod", "rocktrout".

Habitat: Occasionally taken from Puget Sound and Juan de Fuca Strait near rocks, piling, and kelp.

Baits: Mussels, polychaete worms, shrimp.

Table value: Excellent.

Figure 35, Whitespotted Greenling

This greenling is not common in local sport catches and those taken are usually shorter than 12 inches. The WCSDC record is 3 pounds, 8 ounces.

JACK, SCAD AND POMPANO FAMILY (Carangidae)

These are warm-water fishes and although they may resemble mackerel or tuna, they are neither. Like these swift-moving fishes, their tails are deeply forked and their caudal peduncles are very slender. Some very important sport fishes, such as the crevalle jack and permit of the Atlantic coast and the yellowtail of California, are included in the family. Only one species is taken in Washington.

JACK MACKEREL (Trachurus symmetricus) (Figure 36)

Aliases: "Spanish mackerel", "mackerel", scad.

Habitat: A schooling fish of the open sea encountered off the southwest Washington coast from late summer through early fall.

Baits and lures: The entire local sport catch apparently is taken accidentally on salmon tackle.

Table value: Good – commercially canned extensively in California.

Figure 36, Jack Mackerel

Jack mackerel are only transient in our coastal waters. They are strong, swift moving fish and before they are landed, anglers usually think they have hooked a salmon. The maximum length is 30 inches.

MACKEREL AND TUNA FAMILY (Scombridae)

These are beautifully streamlined, schooling fishes of the open sea. They prefer warmer waters than resident fish and occur off the Washington coast during the late summer and fall in the off-shore "blue" water.

Mackerel and tuna have very slender, keeled caudle peduncles, a series of little fins (finlets) behind their dorsal and anal fins and their bodies are nearly round in cross section.

ALBACORE (Thunnus alalunga) (Figure 37)

Alias: Tuna.

Habitat: Occur during the summer and fall in the blue oceanic waters usually found from 30 to 80 miles off the Washington coast.

Baits and lures: In California, most are taken on live anchovies or sardines. In Washington, where a live bait industry has not been developed, most are taken on trolled feathered jigs. Albacore will take other lures and herring baits.

Table value: Excellent.

Figure 37, Albacore

A few charter boats operating from Ilwaco and Westport have been making excursions for albacore in recent years. The usual procedure is to troll feathered jigs on the surface from 80 to 100 feet in back of the boat at about five knots until fish are hooked. Groups of birds in the water and surface swirling fish frequently indicate the presence of albacore. An albacore strike is spectacular and although they do not jump when hooked, and one is very much like another, they are very swift and strong. The record albacore is 93 pounds. The average weight off the Washington coast is approximately 15 pounds. Albacore fishing can be as good off Washington's coast as anywhere.

RIGHTEYE FLOUNDER FAMILY (Pleuronectidae)

The righteye flounders typically lie on their left, or "blind", side. Newly

Figure 38, Rocksole

hatched flounders resemble other fishes, but their typical body form quickly develops and one eye "migrates" to the one side of the head.

ROCK SOLE (Lepidopsetta bilineata) (Figure 38)

Aliases: Sole, flounder.

Habitat: Found in and below the inter-tidal zone over pebbles or mixed sand and pebbly bottoms.

Baits and lures: Polychaete worms, clam parts, mussels, herring, small jigs.

Table value: Good.

The rock sole is the most common flounder in the Puget Sound and Juan de Fuca Strait sport catch. Rock sole, like starry flounders, are aggressive feeders and will often follow and take an artificial spoon or fly near the surface. The skin of the rock sole is rough to the touch.

STARRY FLOUNDER (Platichthys stellatus) (Figure 39)

Alias: Flounder.

Habitat: Common on sandy or soft bottoms in and below the inter-tidal zone. Also, often in estuaries and the lower regions of coastal streams.

Baits and lures: Clam parts, mussels, polychaete worms, herring, small jigs.

Table value: Good.

Figure 39, Starry Flounder

This is one of the most important flounders in the sport catch. They are aggressive and rather indiscriminate feeders and are frequently taken on artificial lures. The WCSDC record is 6 pounds, 15 ounces, however, the maximum weight is about 20 pounds. These fish can be readily identified by their striped fins. About half of the starry flounders taken in Washington are "left handed", (eyes on the left side.)

SAND SOLE (Psettichthys melanostictus) (Figure 40)

Aliases: Flounder, sole.

Habitat: Taken below the inter-tidal zone on sand bottoms.

Baits: Herring, clam parts, polychaete worms.

Table value: Good.

Sand sole are one of the more attractive flounders and can be identified by the several long fin rays extending beyond the fin membrane at the forward

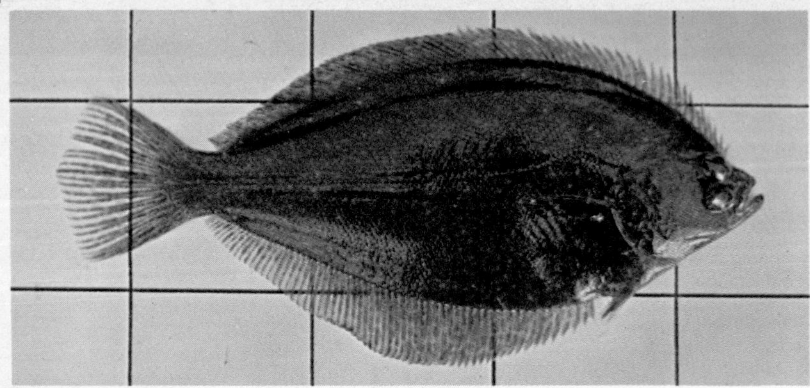

Figure 40, Sand Sole

end of their dorsal fin and their thick caudal peduncles. The maximum length is about 25 inches.

ENGLISH SOLE (Parophrys vetulus) (Figure 41)

Aliases: Flounder, sole, lemon sole.

Habitat: Occur on sand and soft bottoms below the inter-tidal zone, with the largest populations well below the reach of conventional sport gear.

Baits: Clam parts, polychaete warms.

Table value: Excellent.

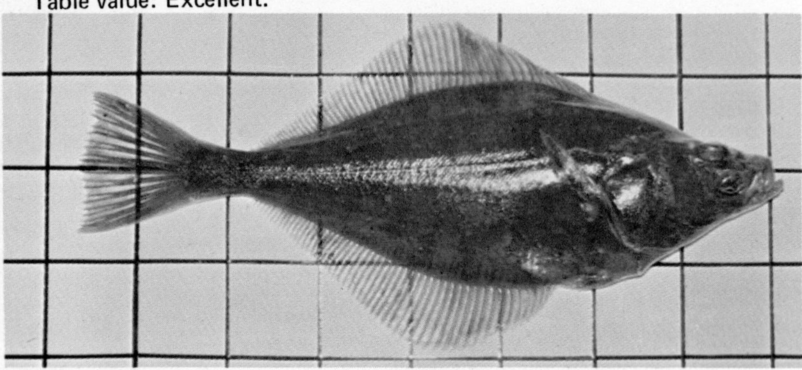

Figure 41, English Sole

English sole are a valuable local commercial flounder. They are one of the more slender species of flatfish taken by anglers and their skin is relatively smooth. English sole appear to be absent from sport catches during winter months.

ARROWTOOTH FLOUNDER (Atheresthes stomias) (Figure 42)

Aliases: Flounder, turbot, bastard halibut.

Habitat: Usually taken over sand or soft bottoms at depths greater than 80 feet in northern Puget Sound and Juan de Fuca Strait.

Bait: Herring.

Table value: Good, however, it becomes very soft if not filleted and cooled quickly.

This flounder can be identified by its large mouth, long sharp teeth, and relatively slender shape. Also, its scales are easily rubbed off. Arrowtooth flounder are frequently misidentified as halibut by local anglers. It is one of

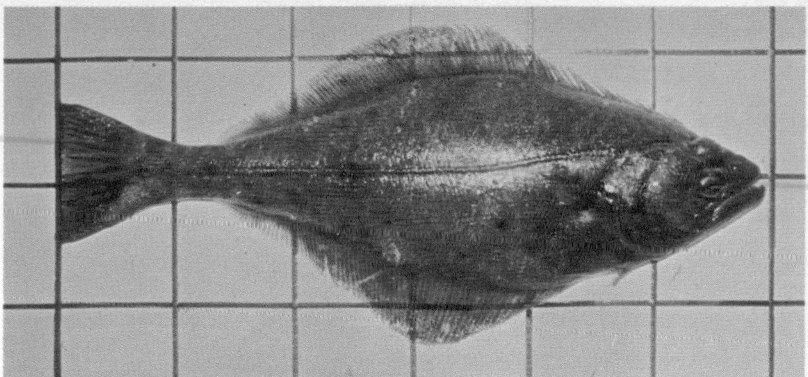

Figure 42, Arrowtooth Flounder

the larger flounders reaching a length of about 30 inches.

FLATHEAD SOLE (Hippoglossoides elassodon) (Figure 43)

Aliases: Flounder, sole.

Habitat: Common in northern Puget Sound and Juan de Fuca Strait on smooth bottoms at moderate depths.

Table value: Good, although it becomes soft if not cleaned and cooled quickly.

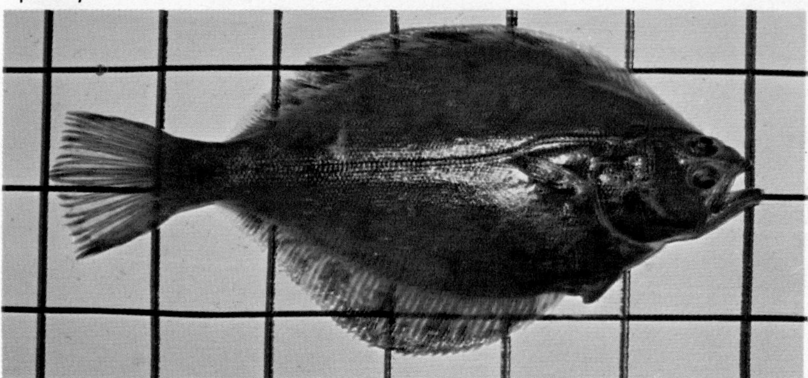

Figure 43, Flathead Sole

These fish are not important in the sport catch. They are similar to petrale in body form, but are generally smaller, have a proportionately larger head, and are softer. Their maximum length is about 18 inches.

PETRALE SOLE (Eopsetta jordani) (Figure 44)

Aliases: Flounder, sole

Habitat: Abundant off the coast of Washington in depths ranging from 180 to 1,200 feet, inhabiting deeper water in the winter than in summer.

Bait: Primarily taken by salmon anglers on herring bait.

A few petrale are taken by anglers in Juan de Fuca Strait and in northern Puget Sound, but the large populations are well below and beyond the reach of anglers. The petrale command the highest commercial price of any local flounder except halibut. The maximum weight is about seven pounds.

See next page.

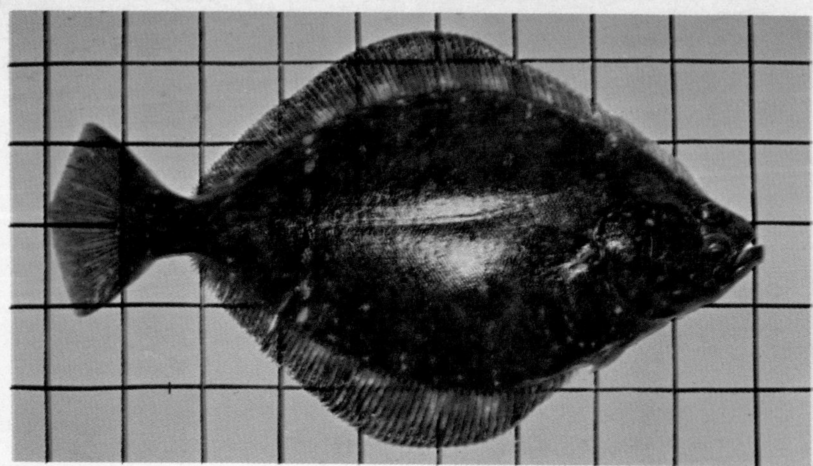

Figure 44, Petrale Sole See previous page.

C-O SOLE (Pleuronichthys coenosus) (Figure 45)
Aliases: Sole, flounder.
Table value: Good.

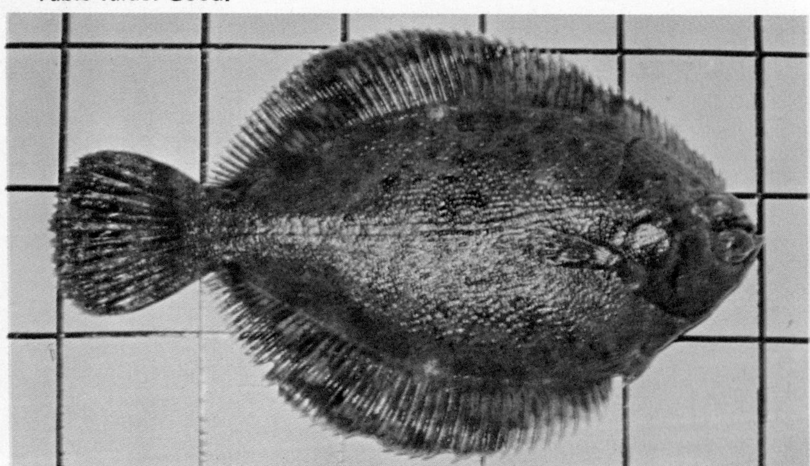

Figure 45 C-O Sole

These fish are uncommon in sport catches and are apparently usually below the range of conventional sport gear. Their name comes from the unusual markings on their "top side". The maximum length is 14 inches

PACIFIC HALIBUT (Hippoglossus stenolepis) (Figure 46)
Alias: Halibut.
Habitat: Occurs on sandy bottoms usually at depths greater than 75 feet from Possession Point, Whidbey Island, northward in Puget Sound, and throughout Juan de Fuca Strait and along the outer coast generally becoming less common to the southward.
Baits: Herring, octopus.
Table value: Excellent.

Figure 46, Pacific Halibut

Because they are so large and good to eat, Pacific halibut are probably the most highly regarded of all Washington bottom fishes. Most sport caught halibut are taken incidentally by salmon anglers. However, they are specifically sought at Admiralty Head, Whidbey Island during the spring and at Dungeness Spit, Green Point, Agate and Crescent Beach and near Sekiu and Neah Bay on Juan de Fuca Strait. The strength of large halibut becomes especially evident after they are boated. Knowledgeable anglers prefer to first subdue them alongside. The maximum weight is about 500 pounds. The largest sport caught fish on record in Washington was a 207 pounder taken off Cape Flattery.

LEFTEYE FLOUNDER FAMILY (Bothidae)

These fish are so named because they typically have their eyes on the left side of their head. Only one species enters the local sport catch. The California halibut, a popular sport fish in California, is a member of this family.

PACIFIC SANDDAB (Citharichthys sordidus) (Figure 47)

Aliases: Sanddab, sole.

Habitat: Abundant on sand in depths greater than 50 feet in central and northern Puget Sound.

Baits: Herring, clam parts, polycaetous worms.

Table value: Good.

Figure 47, Pacific Sanddab

Sanddabs comprise an important segment of the local flatfish catch. They are taken the year round. Average length is ten inches, with maximum length about 14 inches.

pacific salmon spawning colors

With the onset of sexual maturity salmon lose their silvery ocean brightness and each species takes on its distinct spawning dress. The spawning colors of male salmon are brighter than those of the female, and the male also grows a hooked snout armed with large breeding teeth, a "razor" back and an enlarged adipose fin.

PINK SALMON
Female, top; male, bottom

CHINOOK SALMON
Male, top; female, bottom

CHUM SALMON
Male, top; female, bottom

COHO SALMON
Female, top; male, bottom

SOCKEYE SALMON
Male, top; female, bottom
(Jim Ames Photo)

fishing methods, gear & bait

'bottomfish'

Washington salt-water anglers categorize most fish they catch that are neither salmon nor trout as "bottomfish". When angling for these or any fish, the terminal gear (from the sinker to the hook) should vary with the habitat as well as the kind of fish sought. To fish the surf along sandy ocean beaches requires a rod and reel capable of casting a three ounce sinker a hundred feet or so. The sinker should be designed to hold in the surf and sand and rigged to allow the line to slip freely through a swivel eye so as not to discourage delicately biting surfperch (Figure 1). Pile perch and striped seaperch angling from piers or boats in Puget Sound requires a different approach. These are wary fish and since the bait is often held off bottom, a light slip sinker is desirable. (Figure 5).

When boat fishing, the gear shown in Figure 4 is good for flatfish. If a herring bait is used, standard mooching rig is hard to beat and may also produce an incidental salmon. Live fish for bait is both effective and legal in our marine waters and requires a special approach. The hook-up pictured in Figure 3 is recommended for lingcod or large rockfish.

saltwater hookups

Figure 1

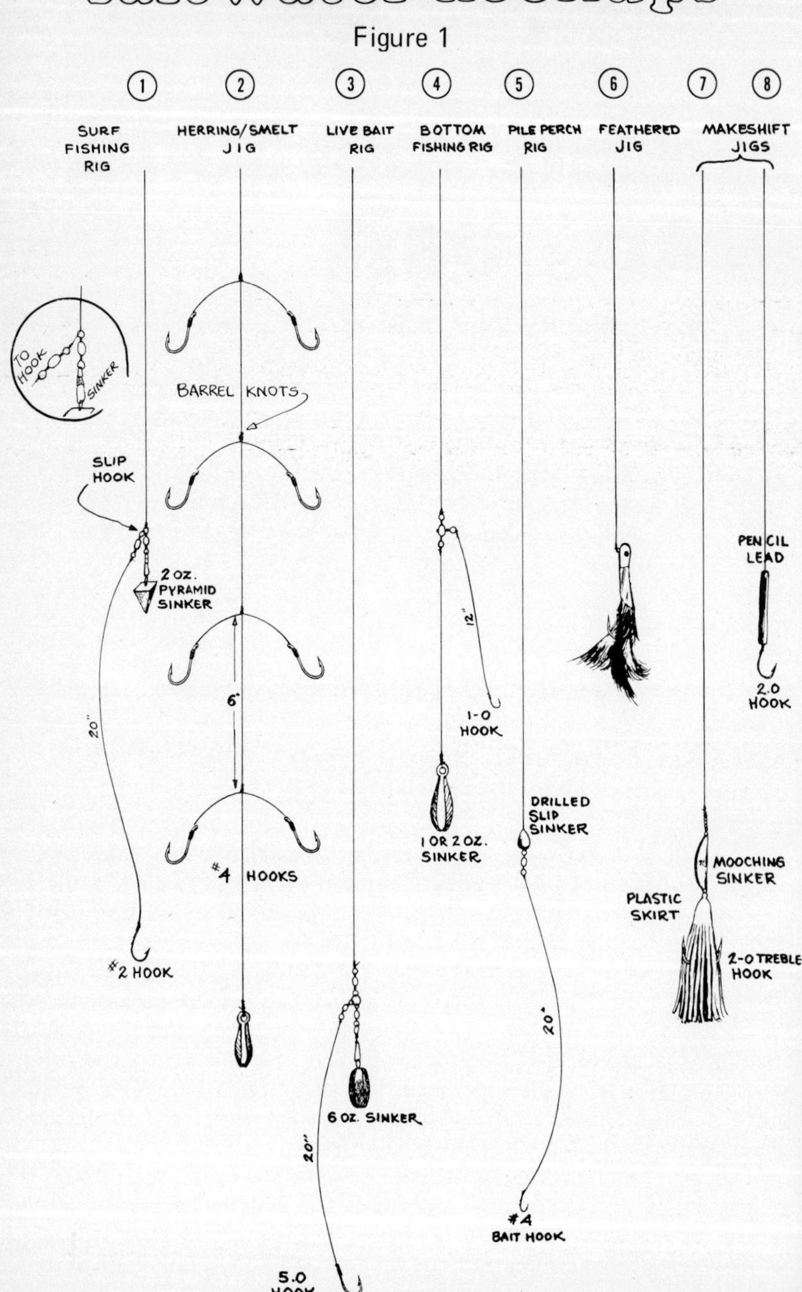

early gear

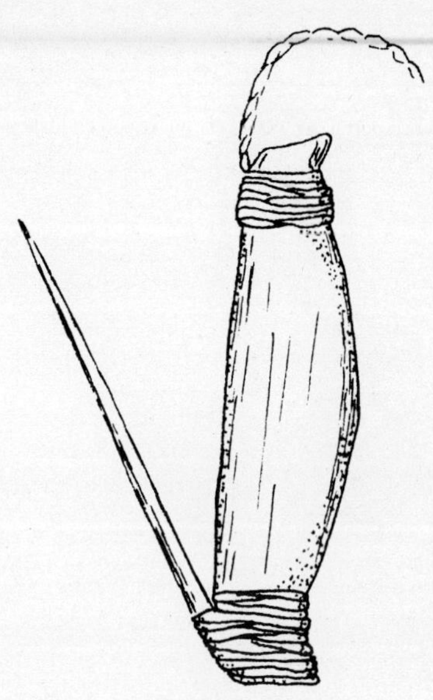

Nootka-type hook used for offshore salmon trolling

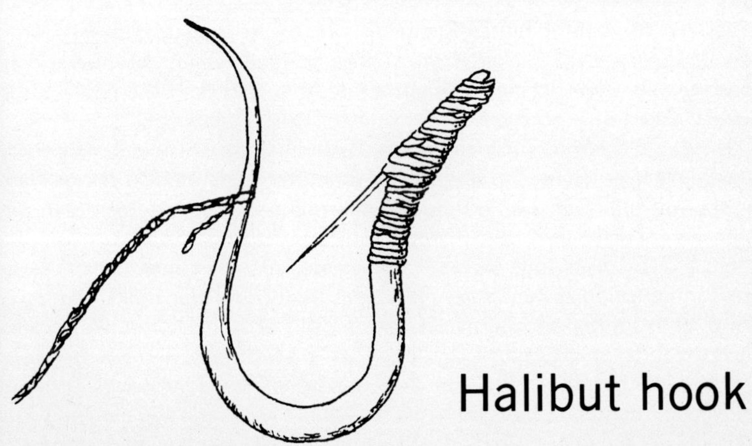

Halibut hook

natural baits Figure 9

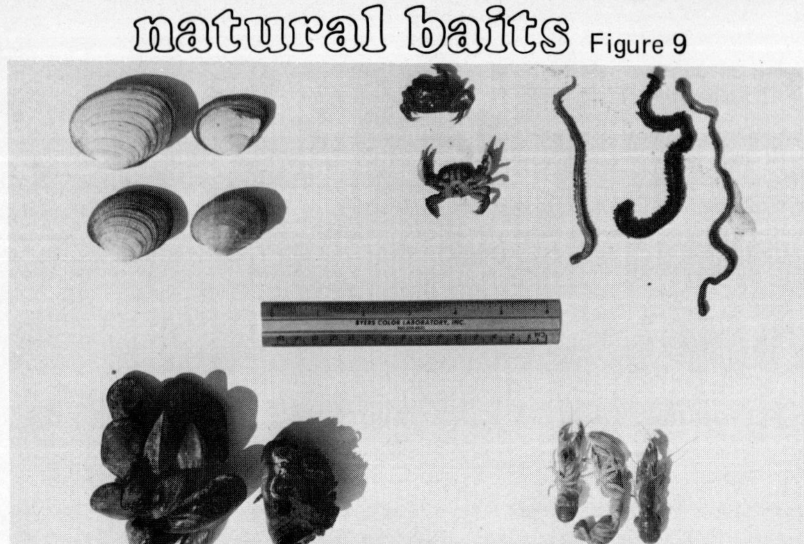

Figure 9. Easy to gather baits. From left to right (above): hardshell clams, shore crabs, polychaetous (pile, sand, etc.) worms, (below) mussels, ghost shrimp.

When fishing from rocks or jetties for rockfish, greenling, and lingcod, jigs (Figure 6) are often best because they can be fished away from "tackle grabbing" rocks and kelp. They are usually cast into a likely spot, allowed to sink, and worked in with a jerking motion of the rod tip. When boat fishing in deep water, jigs are not retrieved, but are simply jerked up and down just above the bottom. The plain lead jig is very effective as shown or it can be baited with a strip of fish belly, fish skin, or pork rind. Plain lead is attractive to fish and it is not unusual to see a rockfish, greenling, or even a salmon pass a bait to strike a sinker.

A variety of natural baits (Figure 9) are easily available to salt water anglers. Mussels can be picked from pilings or rocks when the tide is only moderately out. Even during the highest tide, they may be gathered from the submerged edges of moorage floats or buoys. Mussels are simply broken open and the soft flesh strung onto the hook. Parts of clams or cockles, especially the tough neck portions, are good baits for some kinds of fish. Razor clam necks stay on the hook well during the vigorous cast necessary for ocean surf fishing, and are often sold near the more popular ocean beaches.

Polycaetous worms (pile worms, sand worms, etc.) are superior bait. These worms can be found at moderately low tides by turning over rocks, digging in the sand, or from beneath barnacles and mussels broken from rocks or piles. Some lower tidal species construct long tube-shaped shells and will be found attached to the bottom or the submerged portions of floating docks. Many of these worms are predaceous and are capable of inflicting a pinching bite comparable to that of a large ant. Large worms can be divided into two or more baits.

Any of the shrimp and shrimp-like crustaceans are good bait. Ghost shrimp concentrations can be located at moderately low tides by the softening effect their "U" shaped burrows have on sandy flats. Suddenly sinking to ankle depth in sand is often indication of an abundance of these animals. Ghost shrimp can be collected by digging or by "treading" which collapses the burrows and causes the ghost shrimp to emerge from the sand. At low tide, true shrimp can often be collected from tide pools or from beneath the fronds of kelp and other seaweeds. Shore crabs are another good bait and are very easy to collect from under rocks and debris at most tidal stages.

Herring, although not necessarily the best, is the most common of all local salt-water bait. Packaged frozen herring is available at most establishments catering to salt-water fishermen and some boathouses sell live bait. Frequently fishermen will encounter herring while fishing and if prepared, can collect them on the spot. During late fall through early spring on Puget Sound and Juan de Fuca Strait, certain diving birds, especially the rhinoceros auklet, will cause a school of herring to compact into a spherical mass near the surface. Gulls are quick to locate these "herring balls" and will gather in a tight group above the bait and repeatedly dive into the massed fish. If an angler has sewn a piece of small mesh net (as is used for smelt dipping) into the bottom of his landing net, has learned to recognize the gulls' behavior, and is quick to react, he may have to use restraint not to dip more bait than he can use. More often herring can be collected by "jigging". The jig (Figure 2) is lowered into a school of herring and jerked every few seconds. Herring are attracted to the shiny hooks and either strike or are snagged.

Herring and some other fishes are very good live bait for large rockfish and lingcod. Live greenling, small rockfish, and flounders are excellent bait for large lingcod. Many local fishermen have taken their largest lingcod accidentally when one of these fierce fish has attacked another fish they were trying to land. Frequently, under these circumstances, the lingcod will not even be hooked but will simply be grasping the impromptu "bait" in its mouth – the bait may even be another lingcod!

terminal gear for salmon Figure 10

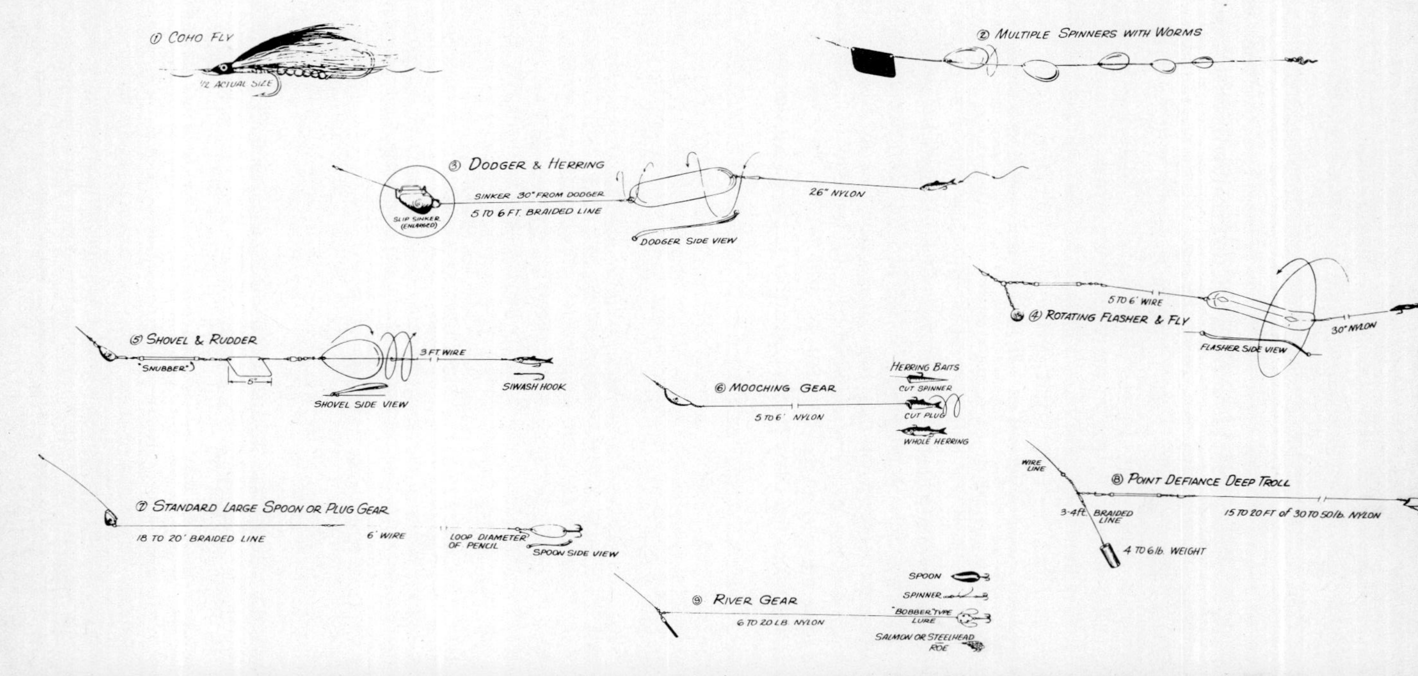

salmon hook knots

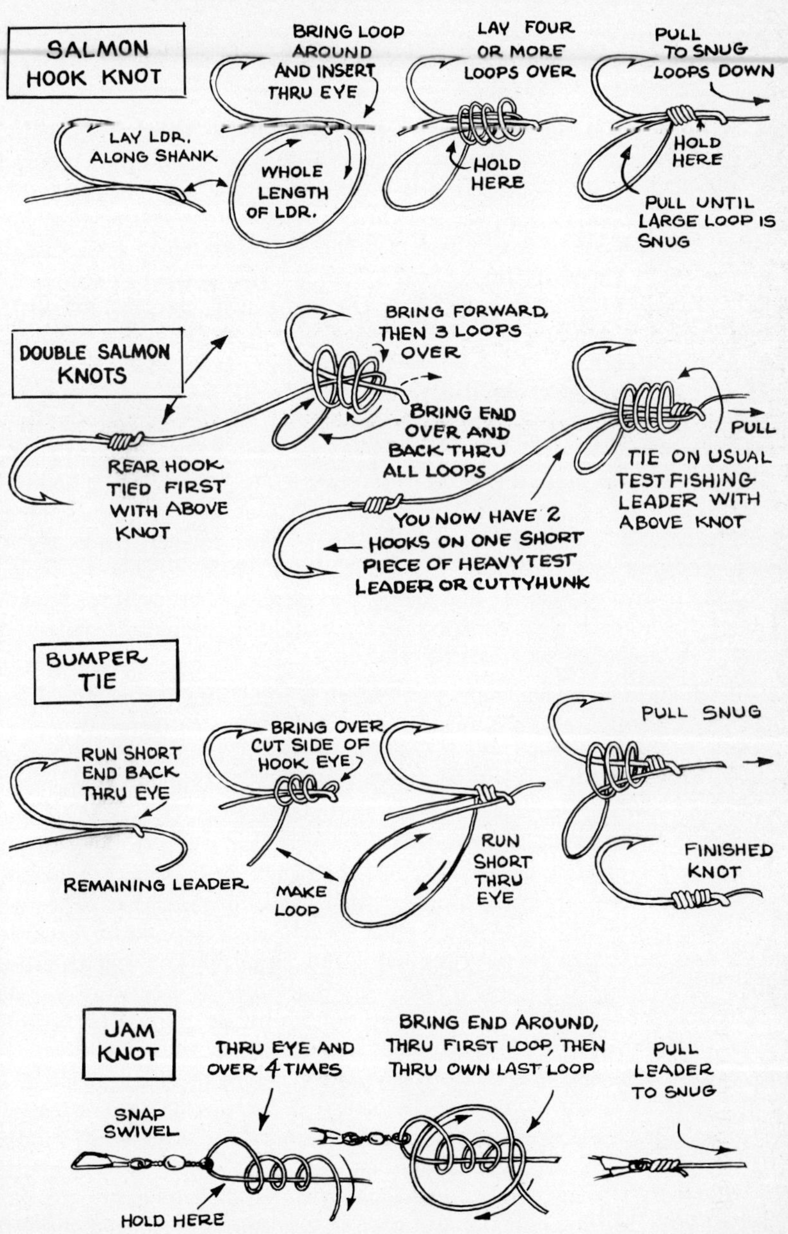

Herring and other fishes can be kept alive in a large container, such as a plastic garbage can, if not overcrowded and if fresh seawater is frequently added. Live bait fish should be hooked rather lightly in the flesh beneath the dorsal fin or above the anal fin.

mooching salmon

Mooching is currently the most popular salmon angling technique in Washington. It is popular because it is effective, involves relatively light simple gear, and it is conducive to groups of people fishing from one boat such as those used for chartering. Mooching terminal gear (Figure 10) consists of a special 1 to 5 ounce banana-shaped sinker usually equipped with swivels at both ends, a 7 foot leader and a bait fish, cut or whole, rigged so that it spins when moved slowly through the water. Monofilament nylon line and leader is used, and most often tests between 8 and 20 pounds breaking strength. Mooching rods range from 7 1/2 to 9 1/2 feet long, have a light action and cork handles consisting of a long butt end, fixed reel seat and short forepiece. Mooching reels are usually light salt water rotating spool models.

Hooks used for mooching range from sizes 1/0 to 4/0 depending upon the length of the 4 to 8 inch bait. Two hooks tied closely together in tandem are most commonly used, with the trailing hook a size smaller. Some anglers, however, think that a single hook is easier to bait, quicker to replace (important when dogfish are abundant), and equally as efficient for hooking chinook if the fish is given time to take the bait. In addition, sub-legal salmon caught with a single hook are easily released.

Mooching requires bait movement which is often attained by the actions of current, wind, and waves on a drifting boat. When fishing from either a drifting or propelled boat, the line angle into the water should be 40 to 60 degrees (Figure 11) for chinook. A "flatter" angle of 20 to 40 degrees is better for coho. (Figure 12). These angles are caused by the difference between the movements of the boat and the water and it is often necessary to use motor (or oars) to attain the proper line angle. This is more frequently the case with coho which are usually within 30 feet of the surface. The mark of an inexperienced angler is too "flat" a line angle (caused by excessive speed) and too much line out resulting in the angler not knowing his fishing depth.

Chinook are found at various depths, but are frequently just off bottom. Mooching gear is effective for chinook because it can easily be fished at a variety of depths and it is very effective while sinking or being retrieved. In deeper water, many chinook take the bait when it is sinking, causing the bite to feel as though the lead has prematurely hit bottom. Often, when wind or tides are too strong, the motor should be used negatively – that is to lessen the natural drift to increase the line angle. When running the motor at a slow trolling speed, shifting in and out of gear, reversing, or changing direction (all causing the bait to fish vertically) are very effective. This is especially true in water deeper than 50 feet. A good moocher fishes the bait vertically as well as horizontally and frequently uses his motor or oars to adjust line angle.

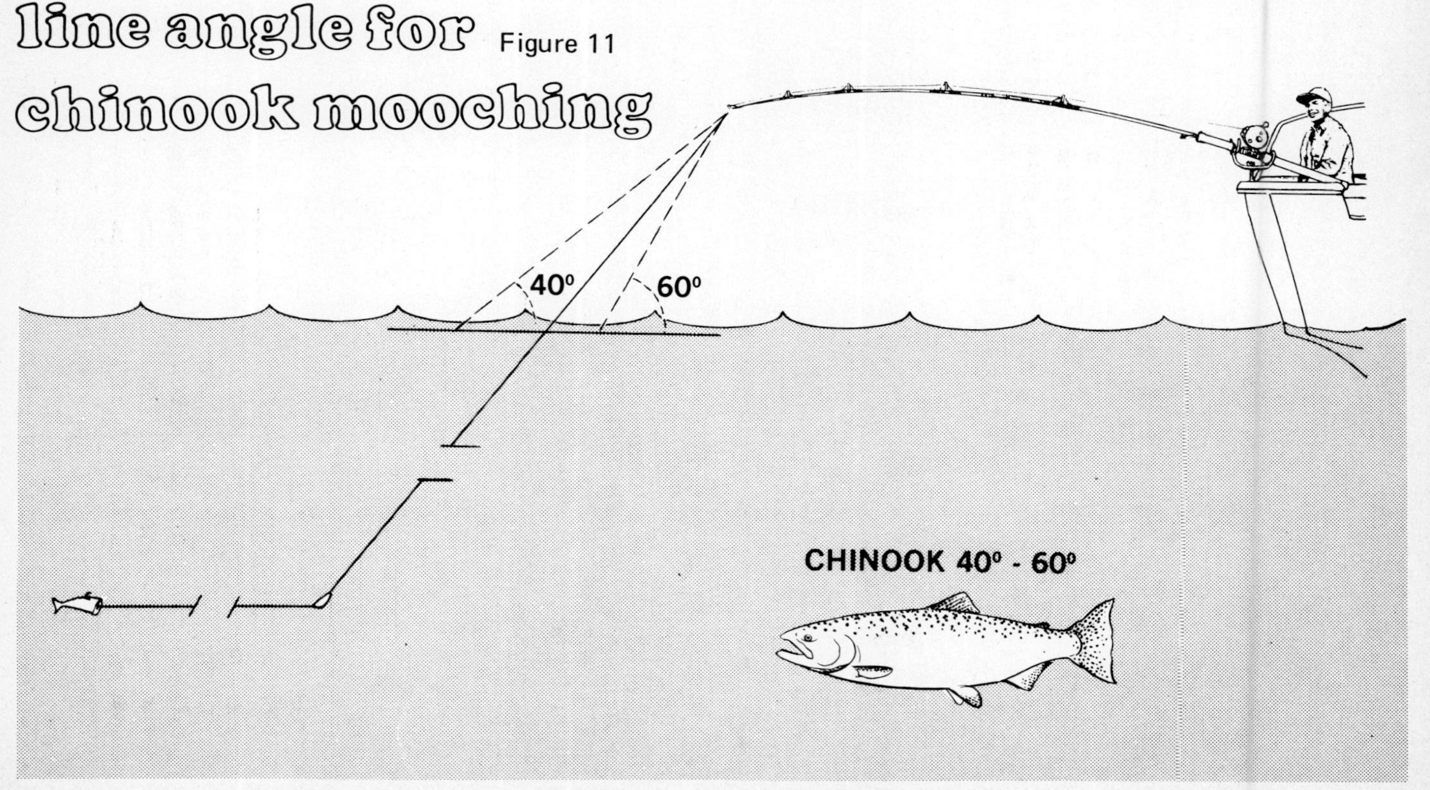
line angle for chinook mooching
Figure 11
40°
60°
CHINOOK 40° - 60°

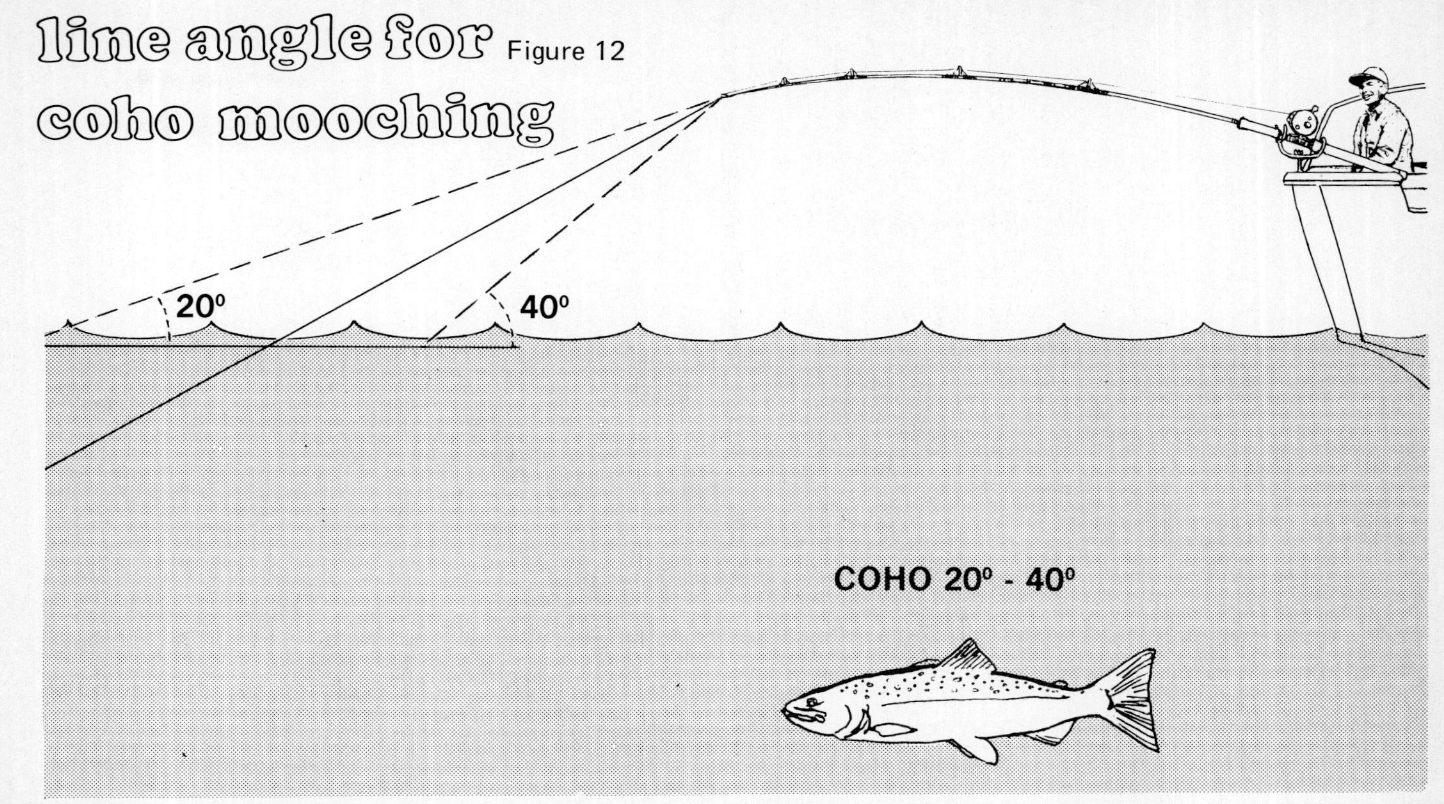
line angle for
coho mooching
Figure 12
20°
40°
COHO 20° - 40°

A typical chinook bite on mooching gear is only a nibble. Usually chinook quickly bite a bait fish once or twice, often spit it out between bites, and then finally take it deeply. At the first nibble, experienced anglers recommend the following:

Immediately "feed" the fish a few yards of slack line, wait until the fish appears to move off steadily and then set the hook by quickly tightening the line (not jerking). Often, when using this method, the fish will move toward the boat and a considerable length of line must be retrieved before the line comes tight. Many chinook are not hooked because the bait is pulled away from them before they take it deeply.

When using a rod holder, the reel should be adjusted so that any tension, in addition to the drag through the water, will take line from the reel. Often the reel "click" alone will serve this purpose. When holding the rod, a thumb can be used to control the line tension. A simple reel and a trained thumb make a good combination.

For coho, the usually faster moving bait and a different feeding behavior results in a more spectacular bite that can properly be termed a "strike". Coho are often hooked when they first take the bait. When using a rod holder, the drag is usually adjusted tight enough to set the hook. For this reason, a two hook mooching rig may be best for coho fishing. However, many are hooked with a single hook mooching rig using the same "feeding" method previously described for chinook. When coho are only "pecking" at one's bait (as they often do), this technique may even be more productive.

How to identify Chinook Salmon

Most COHO have only a few spots on upper tail. CHINOOK salmon have many spots on upper and lower tail.

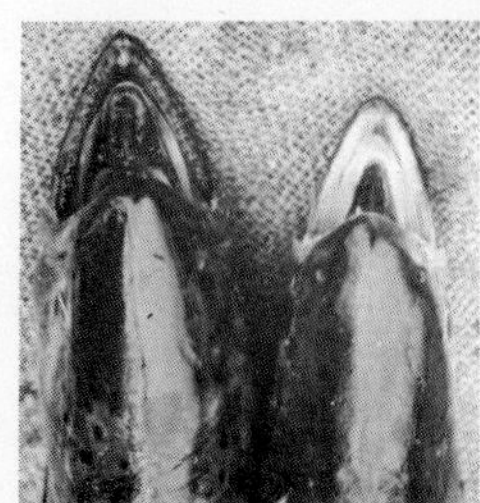

CHINOOK always have black lower gum line. COHO always have white lower gum line.

herring cutting and hooking

There is nothing mystical or difficult about putting a good herring bait on a hook. The following illustrations cover methods for baiting a whole herring, a plug cut, and a cut spinner. For the cut baits, you need a sharp knife for clean cuts to give the finished bait the proper action. Freshly killed herring for whole or plug cut baits are preferred, but the cut spinner can only properly be made from frozen herring. As a general rule, the best frozen or fresh bait is thin ("starved out") because it is firm and is more inclined to stay on the hook. Avoid packaged frozen bait that is discolored or ragged in appearance. Pack fresh herring in ice so that it stays out of the water formed as the ice melts and it lays straight. Herring, thus cared for, remains firm for about 30 hours.

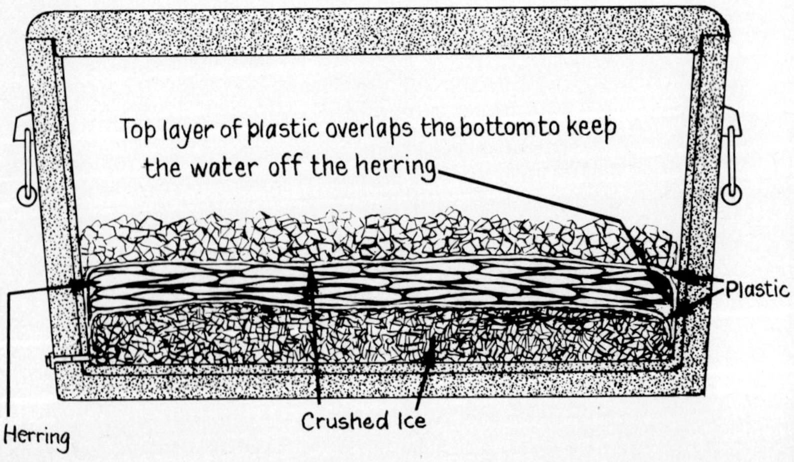

baits

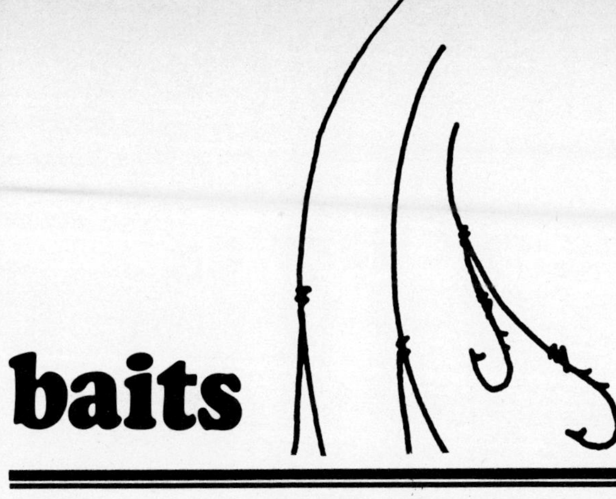

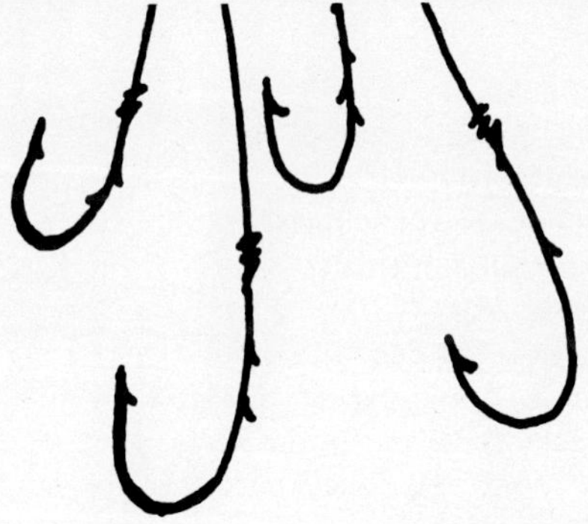

RECOMMENDED HOOK SIZES

Double hooks are used in the following illustrations, but if a single hook is preferred, the same procedure is followed except the trailing hook is absent. The following hook sizes are recommended for the bait size indicated:

Length (inches) finished bait	Double hook sizes Lead Hook	Trailing Hook	Single Hook Sizes
3 1/2 – 4 1/2	1/0	1	1/0
4 1/2 – 5 1/2	2/0	1/0	2/0
5 1/2 – 6 1/2	3/0	2/0	3/0
6 1/2 – 7 1/2	4/0	3/0	4/0

The herring baits described are supposed to spin. Before lowering the bait to fishing depth, it should first be tested by pulling it through the water while in view alongside the boat.

plug-cut herring

Top left, trailing hook. Top center, lead hook.

A sharp knife and a herring are the basic ingredients for plug-cut herring fishing. This is a highly popular salmon bait and is very easy to cut and rig. Plug-sized herring are from five to seven inches long before they are beheaded.

1. Lay the herring on a board and cut the head off, in back of the pectoral fins, at about a 45 degree angle.

1

2. Remove the entrails by trapping them against the cutting board with the knife point and pulling the plugged bait away.

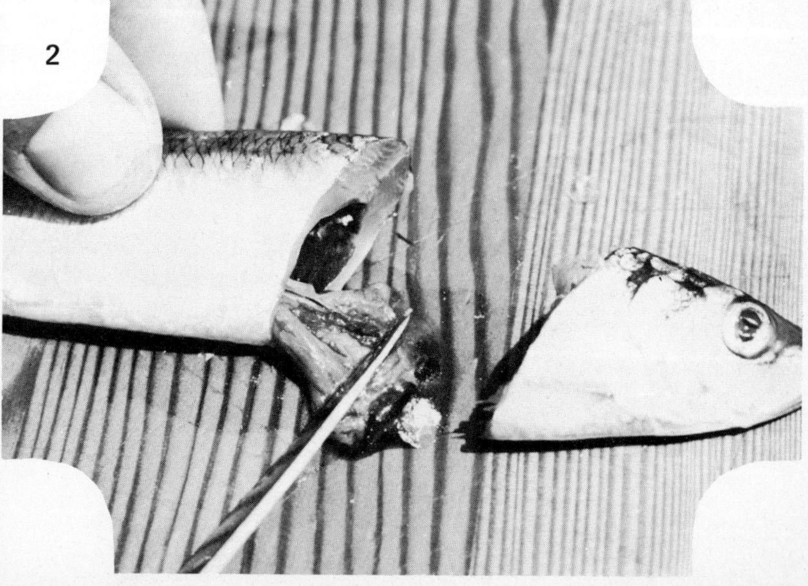
2

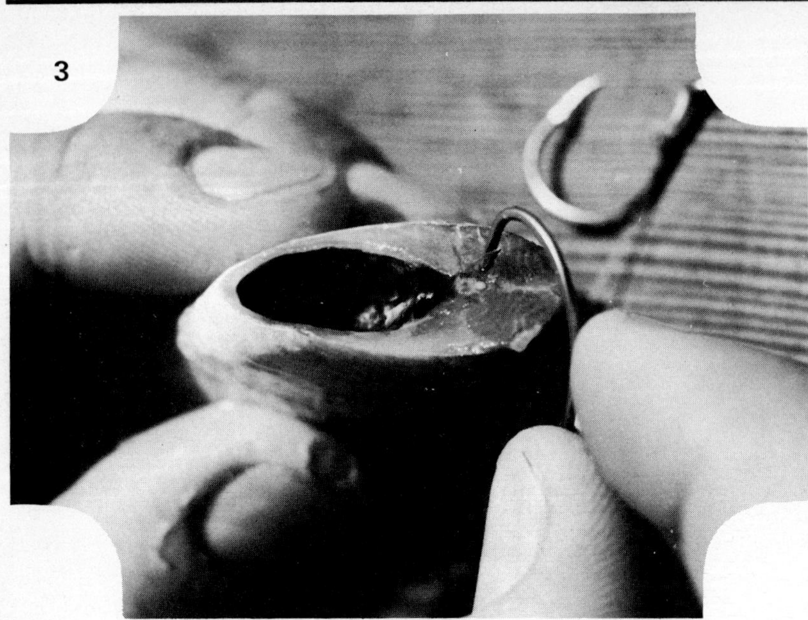

3/4. Insert the point of the trailing hook into the face of the cut so that the hook passes through the spine and out the side of the bait. Pull the hook and leader clear through the herring and follow through with the other hook.

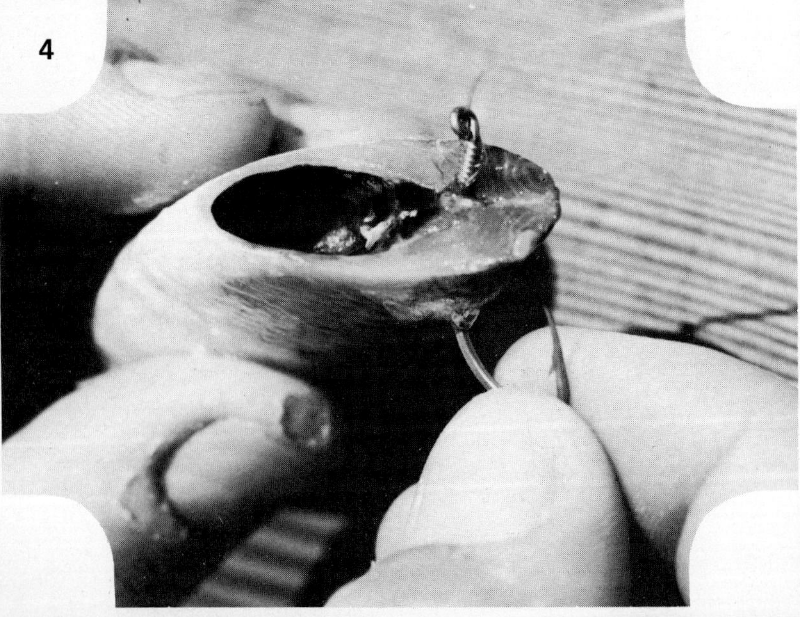

5/6. Seat the trailing hook in the side of the herring that is opposite the side from which the leader emerges.

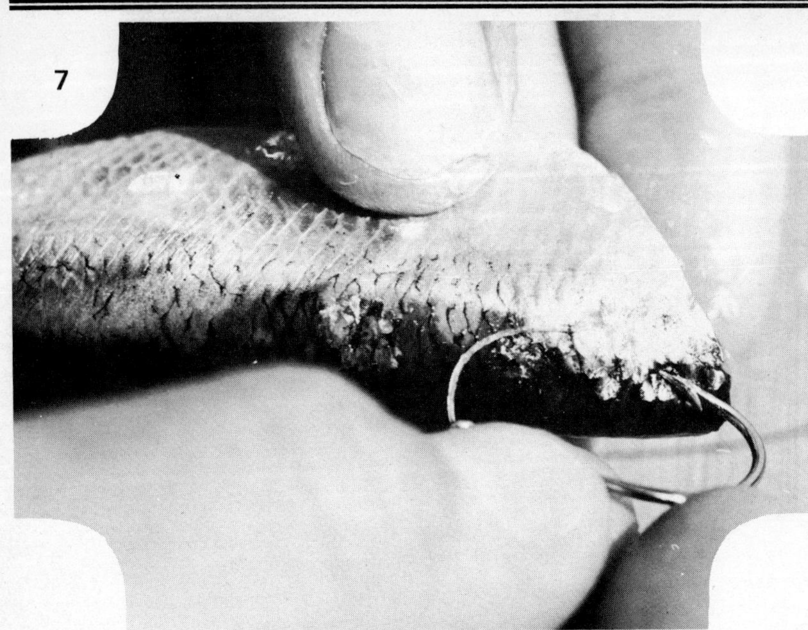

7/8. Seat the lead hook in the other side of the bait. The hook point should enter just in front of where the leader emerges from the skin. Pull the leader gently so as to completely seat the lead hook and the bait is ready to test.

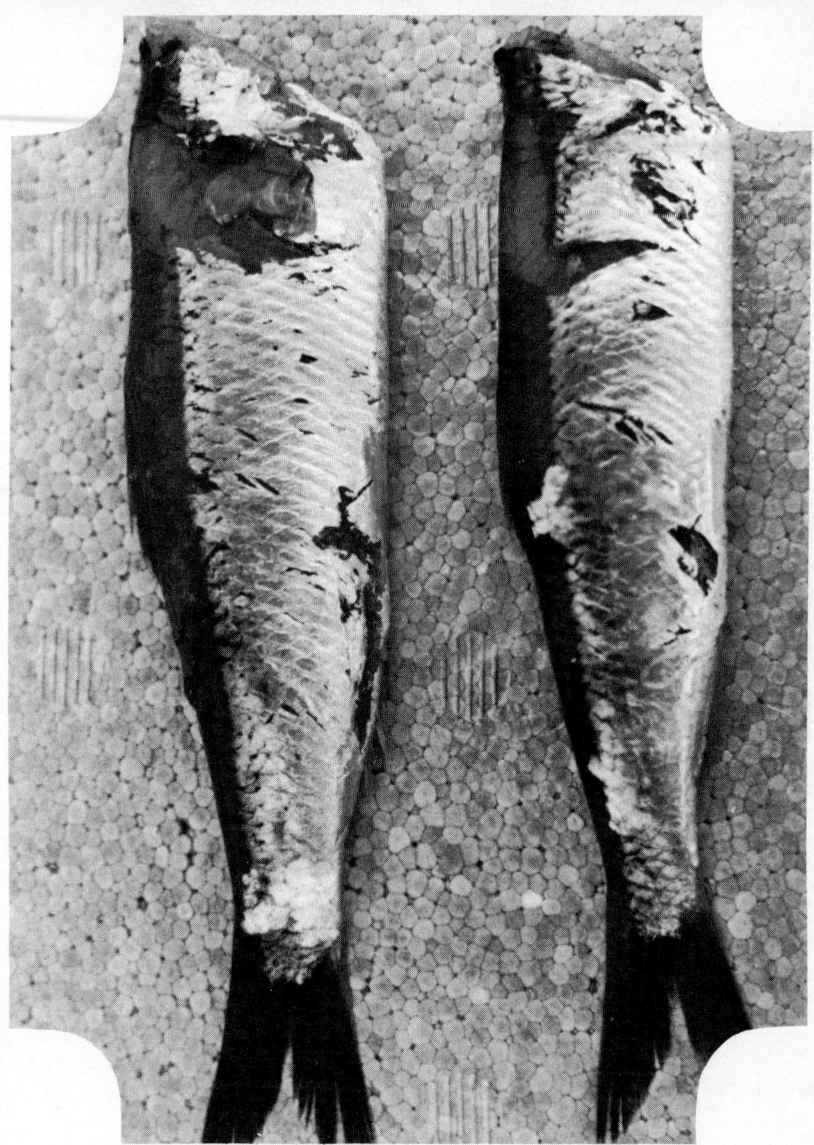

SALMON TEETH MARKS

Teeth marks like these mean salmon! The upper plug-cut herring was taken by a 10-12 pound chinook and the lower bait by a coho of about 15 inches. In both cases, the salmon were observed. The larger fish left well-spaced, deep puncture wounds whereas the small coho tended to scrape the bait. The large open wounds in the front portions of the herring were inflicted by the hooks being pulled free.

This white sturgeon picked up a herring bait in Puget Sound at Duwamish Head, proving that herring will take most any species of fish. It weighed 25 pounds. (F&H News' Photo)

whole herring

Whole herring are preferred when bait is too small, (less than 5" long) or it is too soft to plug cut. A soft whole herring stays on a hook better than a soft plugged herring. Occasionally, for big chinook, large, whole herring are effective.

1/2. Insert the trailing hook's point into the "silt" under the lower jaw and pull the hook and leader up through the herring's snout. Follow through with the lead hook.

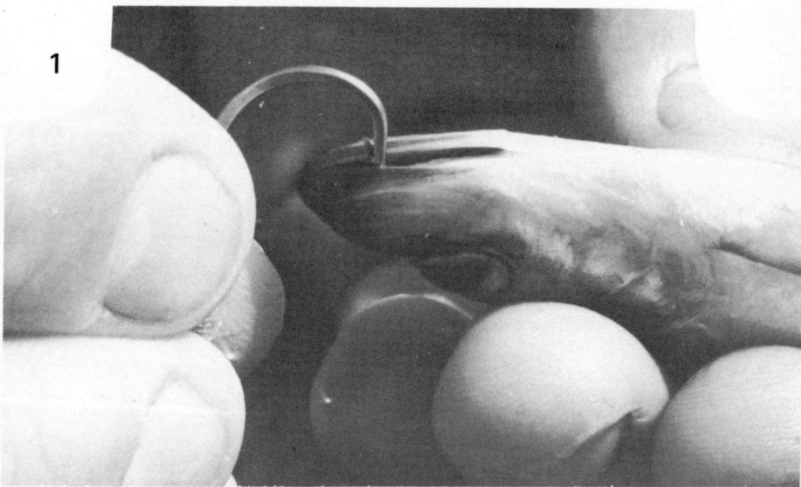

1

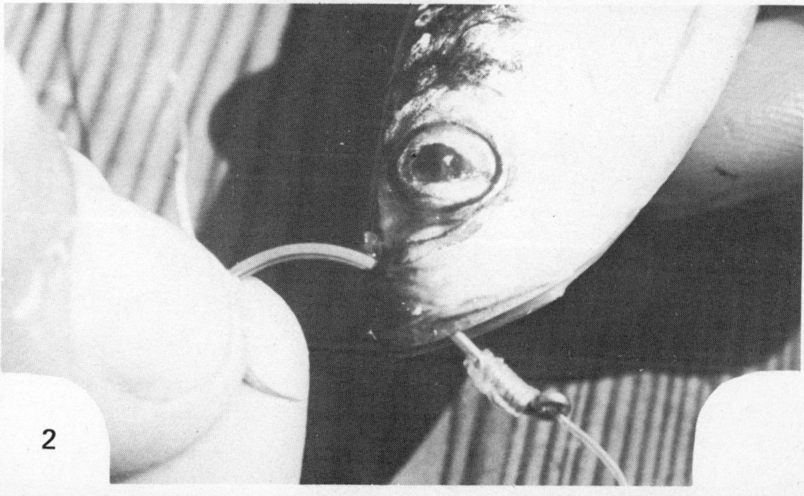

2

3. Insert the trailing hook's point into the upper edge of the eye socket, without damaging the eye itself, and bring the hook point out the corresponding spot on the other side. Pull the hook clear through and follow with the lead hook.

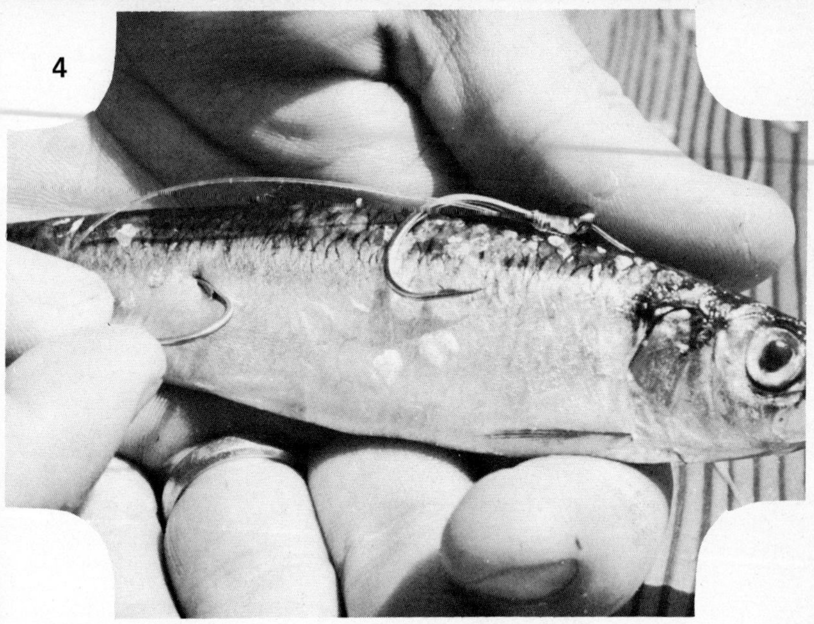

4/5. Seat the trailing hook in the side of the herring that is opposite the side from which the leader emerges from the eye socket.

6. Seat the lead hook in the other side of the bait, near the head.

7. Gently pull the leader in front of herring to take up the slack, and the bait is ready to test.

cut spinners

CUT SPINNERS. Two of these baits are cut from each large (9-11 inch) herring. Consistent spinner cutting requires a razor-sharp knife (especially near the point) and a herring that is frozen stiff. For this reason, spinners are usually cut just before leaving shore or cut and re- frozen for longer periods of time. Unlike the plug cut and whole herring baits, spinner cutting does require a little practice and finesse.

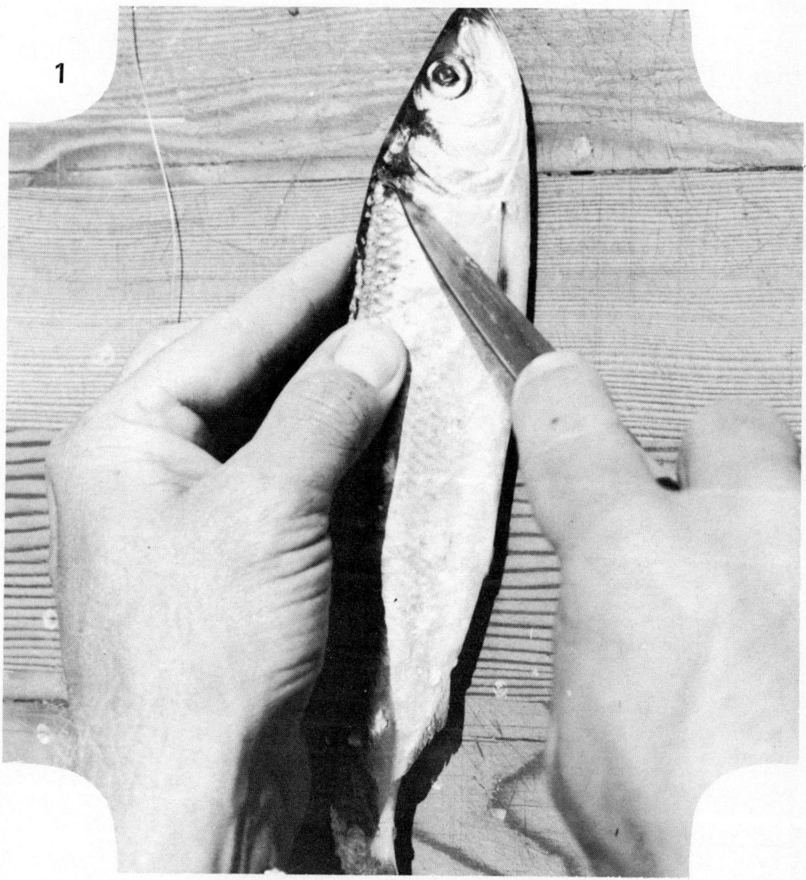

1/2/3. Make a straight cut, beveled at about 45 degrees, behind the gill covers. Do not cut deeper than the middle of the herring. Make the second and third cuts shallow above the belly and below the back.

2

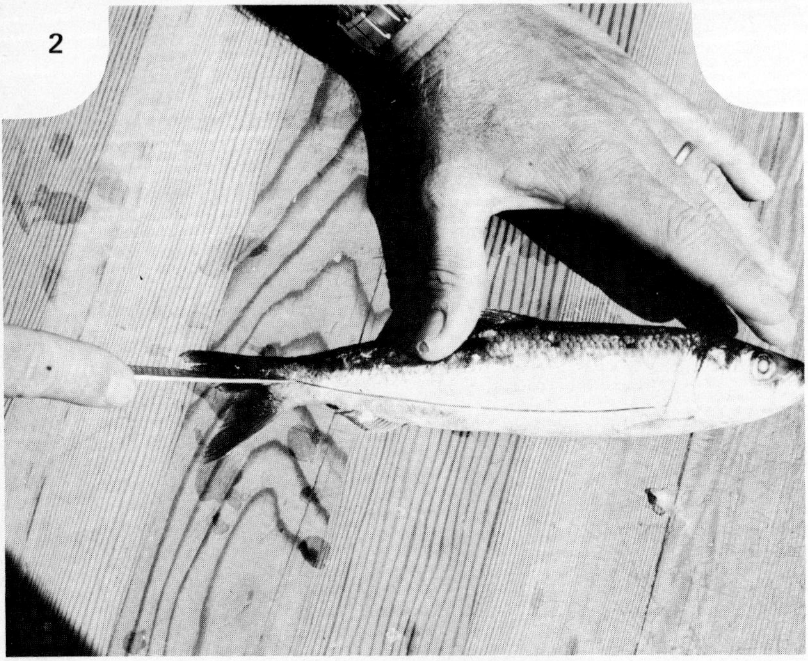

3

4

4/5. Holding the herring against the cutting board, insert the knife alongside the dorsal fin so that the knife's flat side is against the spine, and push the blade through the belly cut. Work the blade forward, while holding it flat against the spine, until it passes through the first cut.

5

6. Turn the knife so that the cutting edge is toward the tail, re-insert the blade into the same cut and work it toward the tail, holding the blade flat against the spine. Remove the spinner and scrape away any entrails adhering to the body cavity wall.

6

7/8. The spinner should look something like this.

9. Insert the trailing hook into the flesh side of the spinner and pull the hook out the scale side. Follow through the same hole with the lead hook.

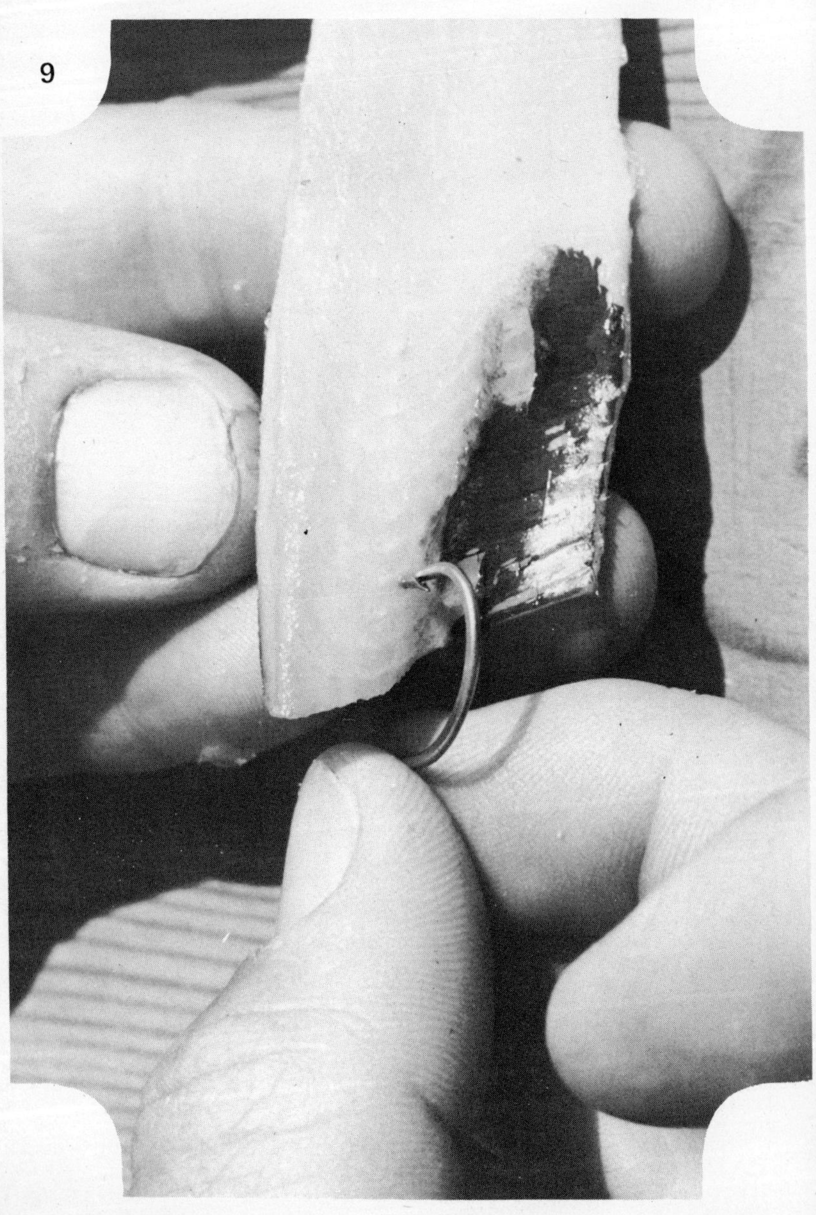

10/11. Seat the lead hook into the scaled side of the bait. The hook point should enter the skin just in front of the hole where the leader emerges from the scales. Let the trailing hook hang free, and the spinner is ready to test.

live herring

Nothing looks more like a live, injured herring than the genuine article. Live bait is used to good advantage by many Canadian anglers, but by only a few knowledgeable Puget Sounders. Ronald B. Stokes of Vancouver, British Columbia, has given advice on live baiting with herring. Obviously, of primary importance to successful live bait fishing is keeping the bait alive. The critical factors are: (1) a suitable container; (2) cool, clean seawater; and (3) adequate dissolved oxygen in the water.

A plastic garbage can, of 20-gallon capacity, makes an acceptable container. Galvanized metal is toxic to fish, as are some plastic containers treated with substances to kill bacteria. A plastic bag type liner should be used if you are not sure if the container has been so treated. The container should only be about half filled with water to prevent spillage.

Water temperature is important when air temperatures exceed 60 degrees F. Herring require more oxygen and space with higher temperatures. The water can be cooled by replacing it with fresh seawater or with ice sealed in a plastic bag.

Like most other fishes, herring must take dissolved oxygen from the water. In order to keep herring healthy in a small container, the water must be frequently aerated. This can be done by dipping water from the bait container, with a smaller pail, and pouring it back from a 2 or 3-foot height. A simple aeration pump can be fashioned from a hand or air mattress pump, by attaching a length of aquarium or surgical tubing between the pump and an aquarium aeration stone. Aeration stones, available at most pet stores, break the air into small bubbles which allow the oxygen to be more readily absorbed into the water.

Experienced live baiters prefer small, sharp hooks. A No. 6 single lead hook with a No. 6 treble hook trailing is a favorite with Canadian experts. The lead hook is inserted near the nostrils with the treble hooked lightly in back of the dorsal fin.

Live Herring Hook-up

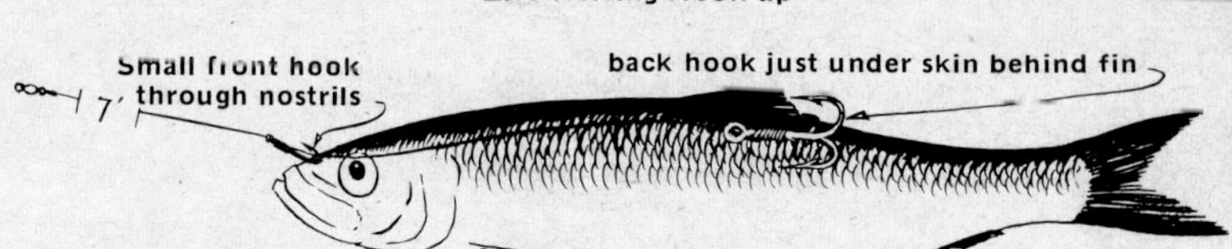

A light mooching lead, weighing about 1 1/2 ounces, and a 6-foot leader and a light mooching rod are recommended. Since the live herring provides its own action, it is usually fished from a drifting or anchored boat. When fishing over depths exceeding 50 feet, the usual method is to drop the bait to the bottom and then quickly raise it about 25 feet where it is fished. At dawn or just before dark, it is usually advantageous to fish the bait within 25 feet of the surface.

A typical salmon take of a live herring transmits only a light tap followed by a slack line as the fish moves toward the surface. At other times, the salmon will move laterally with the bait and anglers must be prepared to let line run free. No matter how the bait is taken, the salmon must be given the opportunity to take the bait deeply before setting the hook. Because of the salmon's habit of moving toward the surface after taking the bait, it may be necessary to retrieve most of the line before it becomes tight to the fish.

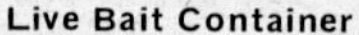

Live Bait Container

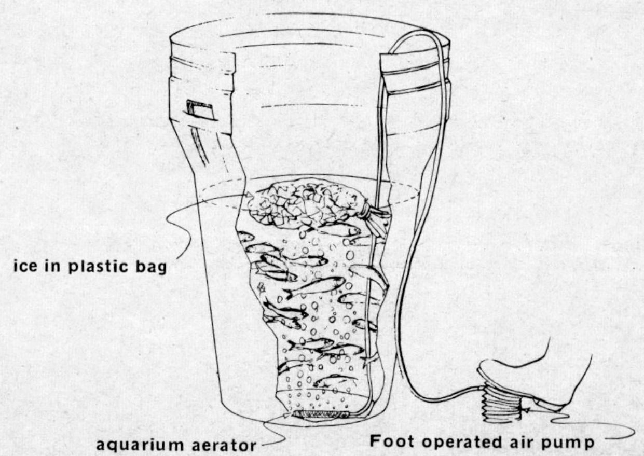

trolling

Some of the popular trolling gear is illustrated in Figure 10. Salmon are usually hooked as soon as they strike trolling lures. The strike is typically spectacular when compared to a bite on mooching gear. A variety of lines, rods and reels are suitable for trolling, depending largely upon the drag of the lures, type of line, and the length of the terminal gear. The trolling rod tip should be sensitive enough to reveal the action of the gear. Proper trolling speeds vary with the gear being used. If one is unfamiliar with a particular piece of terminal trolling gear, it pays to adhere to the manufacturer's recommendations.

Salmon are usually hooked as soon as they strike trolling lures. The strike is typically spectacular when compared to a bite on mooching gear. A variety of lines, rods and reels are suitable for trolling, depending largely upon the drag of the lures, type of line, and the length of the terminal gear. The trolling rod tip should be sensitive enough to reveal the action of the gear. Proper trolling speeds vary with the gear being used. If one is unfamiliar with a particular piece of terminal trolling gear, it pays to adhere to the manufacturers' recommendation.

rotating flasher fishing

The authors recently undertook a program that involved catching, tagging, and releasing hundreds of chinook and coho salmon in the Seattle-Tacoma area of Puget Sound. The program had several objectives but one was to get some idea of how many salmon were available to efficient anglers. In order to do this, rotating flasher gear was used because it is considered to be the most effective sport gear available.

In 43 days of fishing, using four rods and one boat, a total of 1,100 chinook and coho salmon were caught in various locations between Fox Island and Point No Point. This catch included only two or three dogfish sharks and a dozen or so other fishes. This program indicates that the average Puget Sound angler, who currently averages between 0.1 and 0.2 salmon per day, could increase his catch by a factor of 10 by using flasher gear. Those anglers about to give up on salmon because of a lack of success, should first try the methods outlined below. If, after a decent attempt, they are still unsuccessful, perhaps trying another sport is in order.

Rotating flashers are designed to turn over in the water. This action produces an attracting flash, resembling the silvery sides of a hungry salmon attacking a school of bait, and it gives the trailing lure a darting action. "Dodgers" are used in a similar manner, but they are trolled at a slower speed and are designed to "wobble" rather than to rotate (however, when trolled too fast, Dodgers will rotate). A proper rod, reel, line and rod holder are all essential for effective flasher fishing.

the rod

THE ROD – A suitable flasher rod has high quality hard guides, a sturdy reel seat and handle, and is about nine feet long. In addition, it has sufficient backbone to handle a flasher and 20 ounces of lead and yet a tip sensitive enough to dip with the action of the flasher. A long rod is needed to cope with the length of gear between sinker and hook. Attempting to net or gaff a fish using a rod shorter than one's terminal gear is a scene that often evokes the remark:

"He should have brought along a step ladder".

The nine foot Betts rod No. 5318 comes close to meeting these standards and was used in the tagging study previously mentioned. There are, however, other suitable rods on the market.

rotating flasher

Figure 13

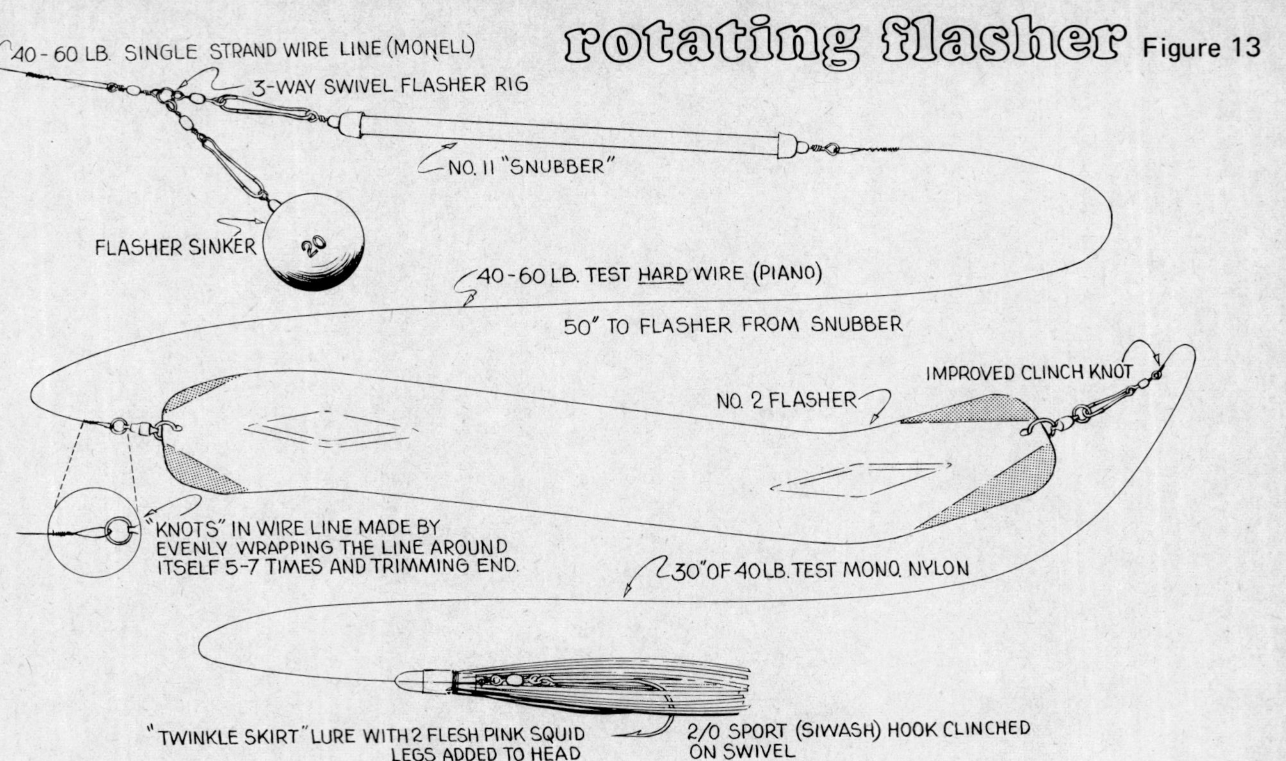

the line

THE LINE - Consistently effective flasher fishing is metal line fishing. Nylon lines are only satisfactory when salmon are uncommonly close to the surface. Not only is it difficult to reach a significant depth with nylon and flasher, but its stretch distorts the "message" of flasher action. Preferred line is single strand Monel of about 50 pounds breaking strength. With a little getting used to, metal line fishing offers no particular problem although kinks must be avoided because they will result in a broken line. Some care must be taken to wind line evenly, and under tension, onto the spool.

the reel

THE REEL — Use of single strand metal line requires a husky, large spooled reel such as the Pflueger Pakron. The Penn 49 is also a favorite among those using braided metal lines as well as single strand Monel (few other reels are suitable for metal line fishing).

the rod holder

THE ROD HOLDER — A sturdy, adjustable rod holder is almost essential for flasher fishermen. The Minzer meets the requirements. The drag of the flasher and lead through the water makes holding the rod uncomfortable for any length of time and if the reel drag is properly set, hand holding the rod is of no advantage. In addition, if more than one person is fishing from a boat, rod holders help keep the lines apart. Flashers are efficient line braiders when fished too close together.

trolling speed

TROLLING SPEED — Flashers are trolled faster than almost any other salmon gear. For this reason they are well adapted to boats that cannot maintain slower trolling speeds. Generally, they should be trolled just fast enough to produce a uniform rotation that transmits a smooth "beat" to the rod tip. The tip dips when the flasher swings low in its arc and raises when it is high. A flasher trolled too rapidly will also rotate and produce rhythmic rod action, but one trolled too slowly or fouled with drift will transmit jerky tip action. One should occasionally check for excessive speed by slowing down to make sure he is just above the threshold speed for uniform rotation. A constant motor speed is not the answer to effective trolling because of changing winds and currents.

trolling depth

TROLLING DEPTH – One of the standard questions asked by inexperienced anglers, inquiring about the details of a good catch, is:

"How much lead were you using?"

This inevitable query is meaningless. Fishing depth depends on line material and diameter, length of line fished, trolling speed, currents, wind, terminal gear as well as sinker weight. The meaningful question is:

"How deep were you fishing?"

Good fishermen know how deep they are fishing and they know how to duplicate and vary fishing depth.

It pays to experiment with depth. For this reason, two good trollers in a boat are usually more effective, per individual, than a lone fisherman. Using the "team" approach, one angler can fish at the depth that is usually productive and the other can experiment above and below this level. When fish are located both sets of gear can be zeroed in on the productive depth. We have often used this technique to good advantage. A fisherman could calibrate his reel so that he can interpret revolutions into line length.

Because of the position of a salmon's eyes on its head and since the source of light in water is from above, salmon are probably more apt to rise to lures than descend to them. It appears, therefore, that a lure presented above salmon is better than having the lure the same distance below the fish. However, because of excessive speeds and poor tackle, the most common trolling mistake is fishing too shallow – especially when chinook are involved. Coho and pink salmon are "semi-consistently" within 30 feet of the surface. However, coho are frequently found most abundant at depths to 75 feet.

A flasher outfit fishing properly.

tips and stuff

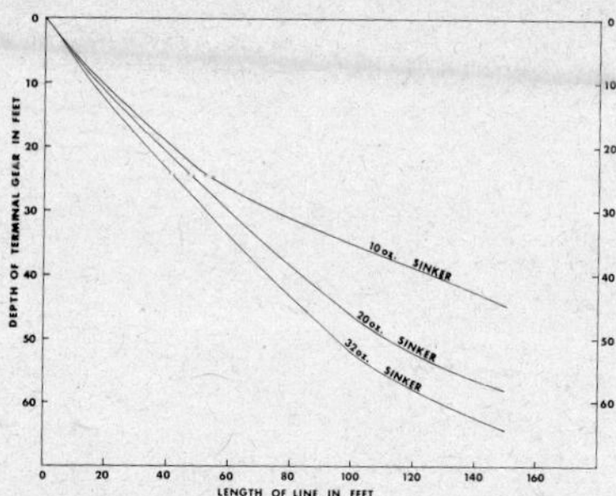

Approximate depths reached using rotating flasher gear (at "proper" trolling speed), from 0-150 feet of .028 inch solid Monel line, and 10, 20, and 32 oz. sinkers. Since a fishing line angle changes (flattens) with increasing line length, the graph lines do not reflect the path of a line through the water - only the approximate depth of the terminal gear using a specific length of line.

PRINCIPALS AND TIPS – Well equipped flasher fishermen will have leads of varying weights to fish properly under different conditions, especially to separate the gear effectively when using the "team" approach. Leads of 10, 16, 20, or 24, and 32 ounce weights will cover virtually all conditions on Puget Sound. For the beginner, a 20 ounce lead is a good all-around size.

The flasher should be let out carefully while the boat is underway and the revolutions of the reel counted so that depth can later be duplicated or varied. The rod should be placed in a rod holder set so that the rod, if not under stress, would be perpendicular to the gunnel and parallel with the water's surface. The drag is adjusted so that a pull, in addition to the drag of the gear, of about three pounds takes line from the reel. The reel click should be on when the gear is fishing, but off while reeling in and letting out line to keep it from wearing out.

Flasher fishing is often ridiculed by light tackel enthusiasts or those anxious to conceal their envy of a good catch. The frequent jibes at this time go something like this:

"With all that weight and other grabage, how do you know when you have a fish on?" or, "If you have to use all that junk to catch fish, I don't want any!"

The fact is that this equipment is so sensitive that an experienced angler can detect even a small piece of drift fouled on his terminal gear. A strike from even a small fish is very obvious and absolutely spectacular in contrast to the typical mooching bite. The sudden and frequent scream of the reel, the sight and feel of a thrashing rod and the absence of dogfish all tend to compensate for the clumsier aspects of flasher fishing. Also, many anglers overlook the use of flashers gear in conjunction with typical light mooching gear. Because flasher gear is trolled rapidly and can fish at all productive depths, it is excellent for exploring large areas in a short period of time. It is often productive in "zeroing in" on schools of fish in new areas, or familiar ones when the bite is slow.

other trolling gear

Fishing the proper depth has, for good reason, been emphasized in the previous paragraphs. Diving-plane sinkers are becoming very popular and provide an efficient means of maintaining considerable trolling depths with ordinary nylon lines. Cut or whole herring baits are most commonly used with these sinkers. Although some diving-plane sinkers can be used with flashers and dodgers, they make it difficult to read the action of the attractor through the rod tip. The strong pull of these sinkers is, however, all but eliminated when tripped by a hooked salmon.

DIVING-PLANE SINKER

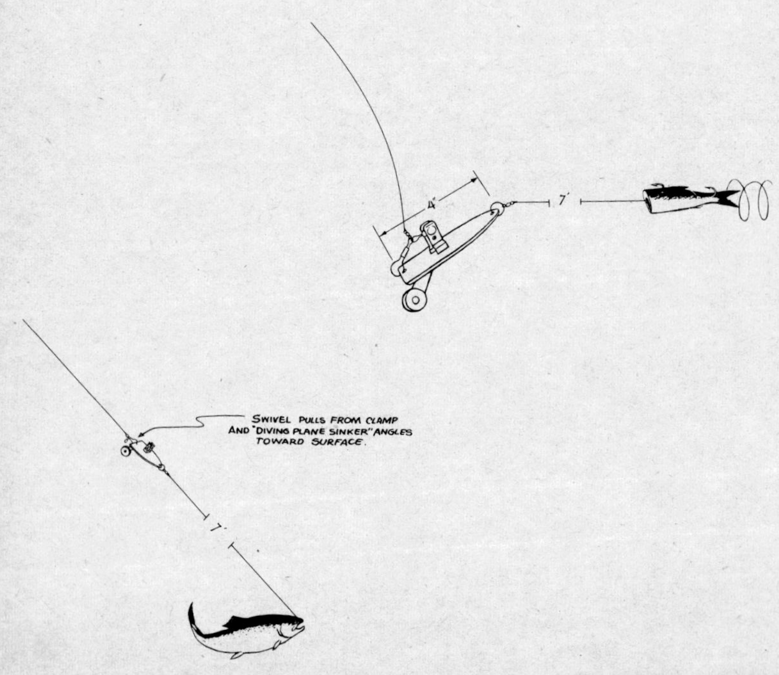

jetty fishing

Popular salmon fisheries have developed on the south jetty at Westport and the north jetty near Ilwaco. Salmon can be taken from these jetties by casting spoons, although herring fished with a float arrangement is the most popular (Figure 14). The float, sinker, and bait are cast out away from the jetty. The sinker then pulls the line down, through the float, to the depth governed by the "stopper knot" — usually placed 4 - 10 feet above the sinker. The float holds the bait, cut and hooked as for mooching (Figure 14), off the bottom where it spins in the channel current.

The jetty herring rig diagrammed is a modification of a rig commonly used. The float is an inexpensive 3" styrofoam ball, purchased from a variety store. A hole is punched through the center of the float with a long, straight instrument of small diameter (approximately 1/8").

JETTY FISHING Figure 14

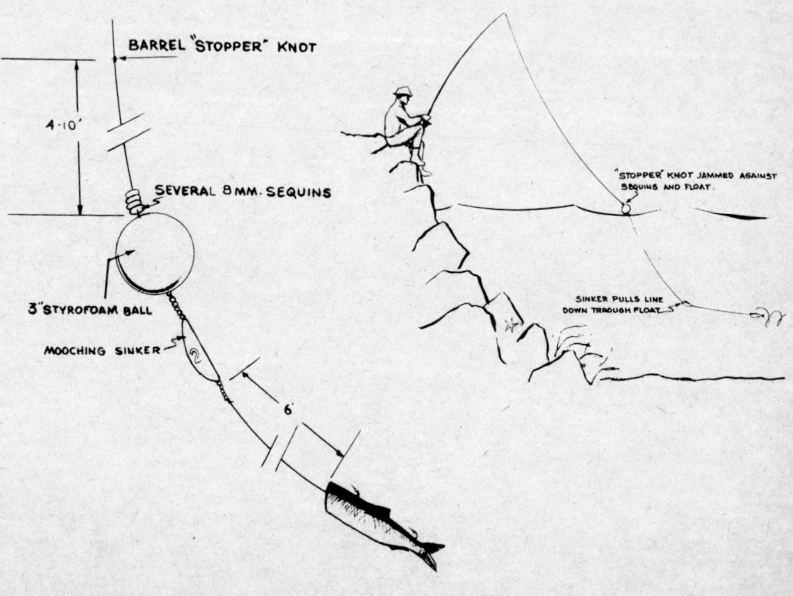

favorite saltwater fishing areas of

salmon habitat

A first impression, after flying over the Washington sport fishing fleet, is how very little accessible water is fished. To some extent, this makes sense because salmon are concentrated in specific areas. However, as one learns about fishing, he knows that concentrations of boats often reflect only the attraction that fishermen have for each other. Conversely, a concentration of salmon is often without an accompanying sport fishing fleet.

Fortunately, salmon are, to a large extent, predictable and one's chances of success are greatly enhanced if fishing patterns are recognized and this knowledge is used to select a time and place to fish. The time can relate to season, stage of the tide, or hour of the

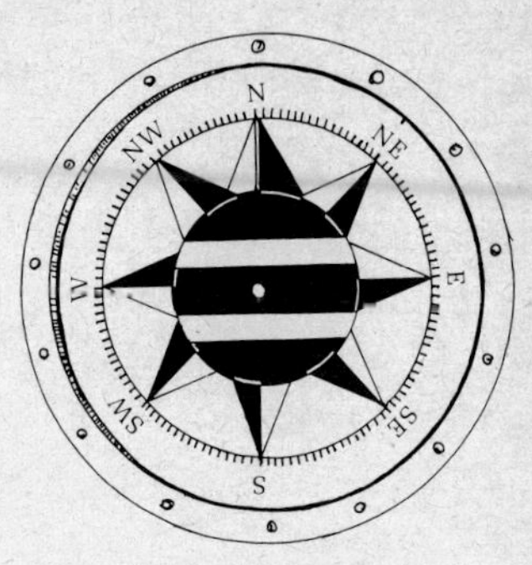

washington

day. For example, a good time to fish Johnson Point (near Olympia) is in May when there is a high tide just before sunset. Salmon may congregate in an area to feed or while enroute to their spawning streams. They are easier to catch when feeding than during the spawning migration.

The importance of selecting a proper time and place for salmon fishing is more critical on Puget Sound and Juan de Fuca Strait than off the Washington coast. Salmon near our important coastal ports appear to be relatively evenly spread over a broad area. This could result from the rather uniform bottom and shoreline that is typical of the southwest Washington coast. In contrast, Puget Sound's many irregularities in shoreline, current, and depth tend to concentrate salmon in very specific areas.

chinook

In Puget Sound and Juan de Fuca Strait, the favorite fishing sites for feeding chinook salmon are usually associated with points of land or other abrupt changes in the shoreline where depths range from 50 to 150 feet, and particularly where there are sudden changes to these depths as occur over "holes" or shoals. Although immature chinook are taken throughout the year, fishing for them on the sound and strait is generally poor in late summer and early fall. However, in winter, it improves when "blackmouth" suddenly appear - even in protected shallow bays where they are seldom caught at other times. Salt-water fishing locations for maturing chinook are usually closely associated with the mouths of spawning streams or the migration routes to these streams. The best fishing for large maturing chinook ("kings") on Puget Sound and Juan de Fuca Strait occurs during the early morning hours of August and early September.

On the southwest Washington coast chinook occur over a broad rather featureless area. During the spring months the best fishing usually occurs well off shore in waters up to 200 feet deep. As the season progresses, chinook are taken much closer inshore so that sometimes the best fishing may be just outside the surf line.

coho

Fishing locations for feeding coho on Puget Sound and Juan de Fuca Strait are usually further offshore than those for chinook and they are more noticeably associated with tide rips. Spring and summer fishing for coho salmon on Puget Sound depends largely on fish that remain inside the sound throughout their lives. These "resident" fish are typically smaller than coho inhabiting the open ocean, averaging about five pounds at maturity. Ocean-reared coho are usually abundant in Puget Sound during September and October, but these fish are not feeding heavily and are usually difficult to catch. On Juan de Fuca Strait, coho angling is dependent on the immigration of maturing fish during late summer and early fall, but occasionally feeding fish provide good fishing as early as July as far east as Port Angeles. At the western entrance to Juan de Fuca Strait feeding coho are usually abundant throughout the summer.

Along the southwest Washington coast the best coho fishing typically occurs in the waters further offshore than those fished for chinook. This rule generally holds throughout the summer, but coho salmon are also taken closer to shore as the season progresses.

pink

An important part of the odd-numbered years sport catch in Juan de Fuca Strait and northern Puget Sound is the taking of "Humpies." Fishing is limited to the migration routes from the open ocean to spawning streams. An interesting exception is a group of fish that spends its salt-water life within Puget Sound. These fish, typically much smaller than ocean-reared pink salmon, have been very scarce in recent years.

fishing maps

...where the action is

olympia to seattle

figure 1

SALMON AREAS

1. DOUGAL POINT - Chinook from late winter through spring. Dogfish make mooching difficult. Access: Boat ramps at Graham and McLane Cove on Pickering Passage; Grapeview and Allyn.

2. STEAMBOAT ISLAND Chinook from spring through early summer with April and May the best months. Early morning fishing and tide changes usually produce the best results. The west side of Totten Inlet is usually best around low tide. Dogfish are abundant and make mooching difficult. Access: Boat ramps at Arcadia Point and Boston Harbor (north of Olympia); hoists in Olympia.

3. "STEVE'S SLOT" - COOPER POINT - Both yield chinook from late winter through spring. Dogfish are troublesome to moochers. Access: See 2 and 4.

4. JOHNSON POINT - Fine mooching and trolling for chinook

from April through June. Fish the area west of Johnson Point during the late stages of the flood tide and southeast of the Point during the ebb. Access: Boat ramps, hoists and rental boats near the point.

5. DEVIL'S HEAD - Chinook from winter through spring. Access: See 2 and 4.

6. ANDERSON ISLAND - Fine year round fishing for chinook. Ebb tides usually produce best from late fall through winter and flood tides during the warmer months. The area adjacent to the Nisqually River Delta yields some maturing chinook and coho from late summer through early fall. Access: Boat ramp, hoist and rental boats at Steilacoom.

7. EAGLE ISLAND - Chinook primarily during the winter and spring months. Access: See 6 and 9.

8. TOLIVA SHOAL - Chinook, coho, and pink salmon are taken in the tide rips by trollers during the late stages of the spring flood tides. This is currently the principal fishing area for the small pink salmon ("humpies") that remain in Puget Sound. Access: See 6.

9. GIBSON POINT - FOX POINT - Year round trolling and mooching areas for chinook salmon. Access: Boat ramps, hoists and rental boats south of Narrows Bridge between 6th Avenue and Day Island.

10. WOLLOCHET BAY - Year round area for chinook and coho (spring-early summer) with chinook fishing best in December. Dogfish can make mooching difficult. Access: See 9; ramp at Wollochet and Horsehead Bays, and at Fox Island.

11. SANDSPIT - A fine year round mooching and trolling area for chinook and coho during the spring and early summer. Access: See 10.

12. "GALLAGHAN'S HEAD" Produces chinook year round. Access: See 10.

13. ROSEDALE - The narrow 10 to 12 fathom slot along the northwest sides of Raft and Cutts Islands produces some nice chinook during the winter months. Access: See 9; ramp at Wollochet and Horsehead Bays.

14. MINTER CREEK - Popular from late summer through early fall for maturing chinook and coho returning to the Department of Fisheries hatchery. Early mornings are best. Access: See 10; ramps at Wuana and Glen Cove.

15. PURDY - A productive mooching area for chinook from late fall through early spring. Early morning or evening high tides are usually best. Access: See 14.

16. POINT EVANS - A very popular winter ebb tide mooching area for chinook. Access: See 9; ramps and rental boats at Point Defiance, ramp and hoists at Gig Harbor.

17. POINT DEFIANCE - One of the most popular fishing areas in Puget Sound during the spring and summer months. Feeding and maturing chinook and some coho. Usually best during May and June around change of tide. Access: Boat ramp and rental boats at Point Defiance Park; hoist, ramps and rental boats on Commencement Bay.

18. POINT DALCO - Yields some husky chinook the year round during flood tides. Access: See 17.

19. QUARTERMASTER HARBOR - Small and medium sized chinook are usually abundant from late fall through winter. Access: See 17.

20. COMMENCEMENT BAY AND BROWNS POINT - Maturing chinook and pink salmon from August through mid-September; coho in September and October.

Early morning fishing is usually best. Access: See 17; hoist at Redondo; ramp at Saltwater State Park.

21. REDONDO - Feeding chinook during the winter months; a few maturing pink and coho salmon from August through early October. Access: See 20.

22/23. CAMP SEALTH AND POINT RICHMOND - During the winter months, chinook salmon are attracted to the tide rips that form at these locations. Access: Hoists, ramp at Gig Harbor; see 17.

24. ALLEN BANK - An abundance of baitfish and other food attracts good numbers of husky chinook during the winter and early spring months. Access: Boat ramp at Harper; ramp and hoist at Southworth; ramps and hoists on Elliott Bay (Seattle).

25. MANCHESTER - Offers trolling for feeding chinook during the winter months. Access: See 24.

26. PORT ORCHARD - Feeding chinook from late fall through early winter. Access: Boat ramps and hoists at Bremerton and Port Orchard.

BOTTOM FISH

Sablefish, copper rockfish, and rock sole are the most heavily utilized bottom fish between Elliott Bay and Des Moines. The best rockfish catches appear to be made in the vicinity of the south end of Bainbridge Island. Sablefish and rock sole are wide spread. Pile perch and striped seaperch are abundant near most of the piers in the area and wherever there are heavy growths of mussels and barnacles.

From Tacoma southward to Anderson Island, copper and other rockfish and Pacific cod are common in catches. The most productive area for these fish is in the Tacoma Narrows. A variety of fine fish, not abundant elsewhere in the lower sound, are taken here: lingcod, black and yellowtail rockfish, bocaccio and even canary rockfish are taken in good numbers. The sunken evirons of the original Tacoma Narrows Bridge is home for many rockfish and lingcod. Good rockfish grounds are also on Toliva Shoal. Pile perch and striped seaperch are abundant throughout the area. During the late fall and winter, large numbers of Pacific cod are jigged off the bottom in the 20 fathom region just south of Point Fosdick.

Case Inlet and the waters in the vicinity of Olympia have relatively little to offer the non-salmon angler except for pile perch, striped seaperch, and rock sole.

TROUT

Cutthroat trout are taken along many miles of shoreline between Seattle and Olympia. Some of the more popular areas are the west side of Colvos Passage, the north side of Hale Passage, Horsehead Bay on Carr Inlet (in the vicinity of Purdy), the west shoreline of the Long Branch Peninsula, the southeast shoreline of Hartstene Island, and in most of the other inlets in the vicinity of Olympia.

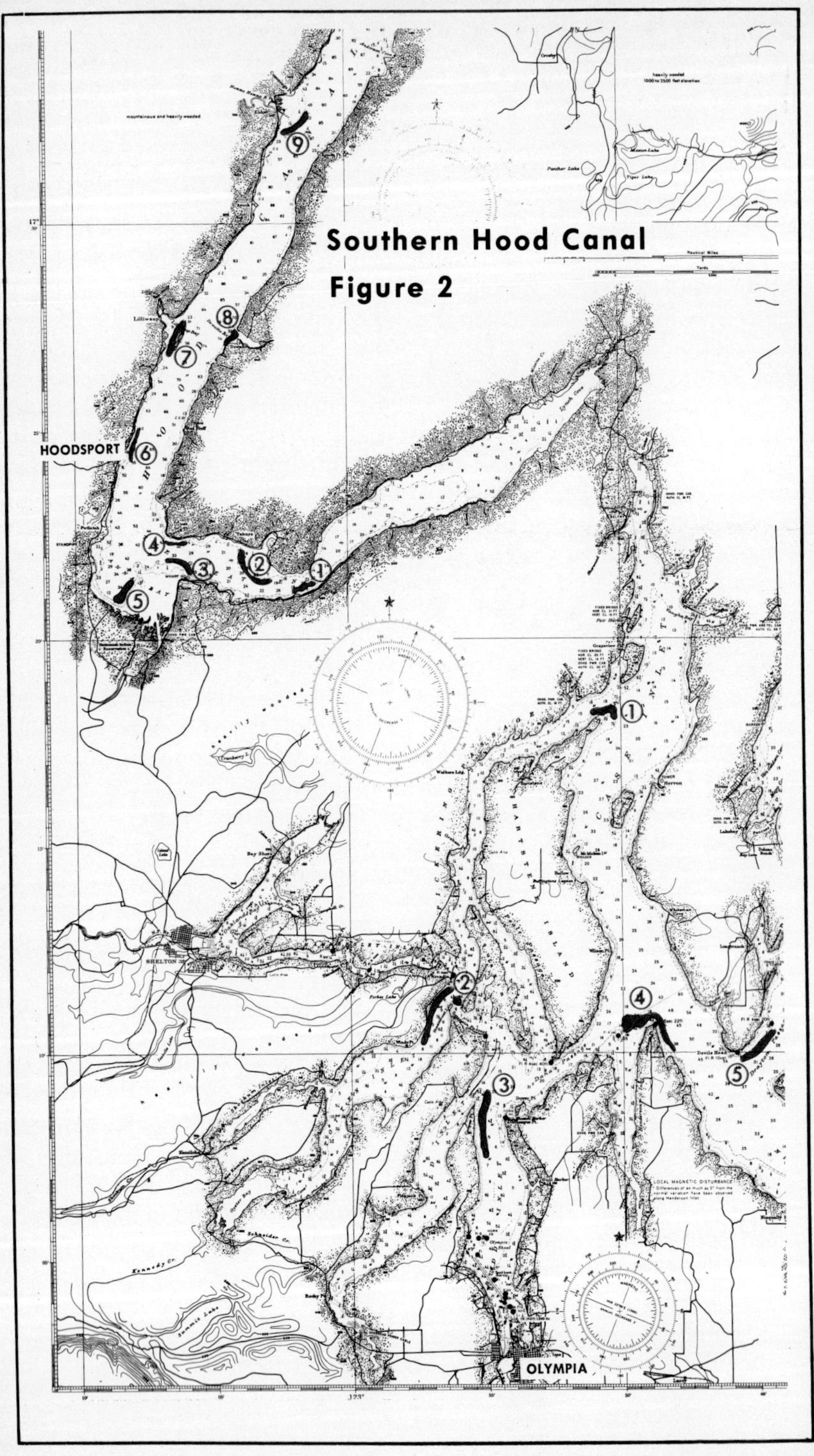
Southern Hood Canal
Figure 2
HOODSPORT
SHELTON
OLYMPIA
Lilliwaup
mountainous and heavily wooded
LOCAL MAGNETIC DISTURBANCE

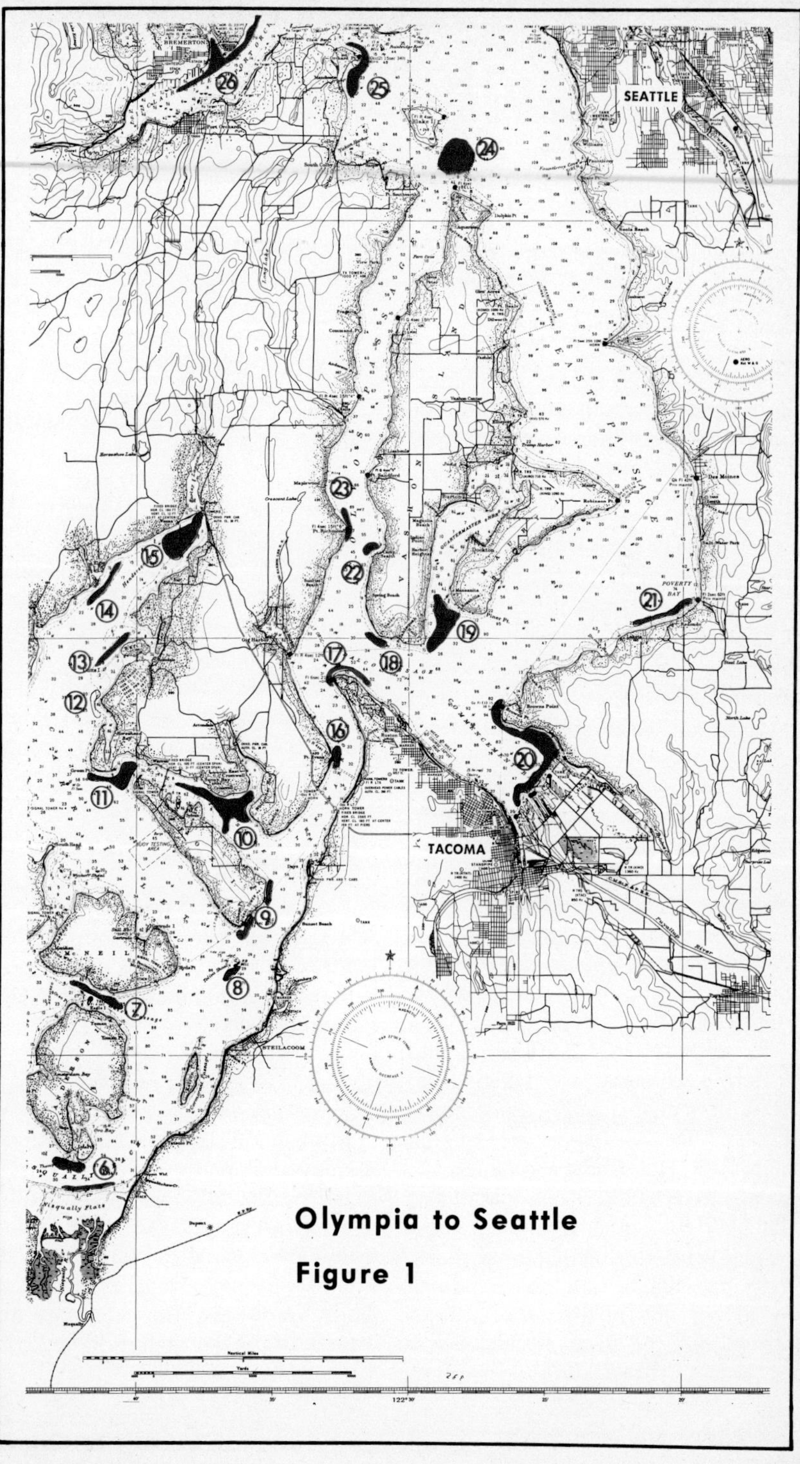

Olympia to Seattle

Figure 1

southern hood canal

figure 2

SALMON AREAS

1. CHICKEN HOLE - Produces some large feeding chinook during the winter months. Access: Ramps and hoist at Union; ramps at Tahuya and at Belfair and Twanoh State Parks.

2. TAHUYA - Maturing coho are taken from mid-September through October. Access: See 1.

3. UNION - Feeding and maturing chinook are taken during the morning ebb tide along the northeast edge of the Skokomish Delta from May through early September. Maturing coho are available from mid-September through October. Access: See 1.

4. BALD POINT - Feeding and maturing chinook are taken from March through early September. The best fishing time appears to be during the early morning flood tides. Access: See 1.

5. INDIAN HOLE - Feeding and maturing chinook are taken from May through early September. Access: See 1; ramps at Potlatch State Park, Hoodsport and Union.

6. HOODSPORT - Maturing hatchery chinook and coho are taken from August through October. Early morning hours are best. Some feeding chinook are taken throughout the year. Access: See 5 hoist, ramp at Restwhile Park (north of Hoodsport).

7. DEWATTO - Produces large, maturing coho from late September through early November. Access: See 6.

8. LILLIWAUP - Feeding chinook and coho are taken during the spring and summer months. Access: See 6; private boat ramp at Mike's Beach (north of Lilliwaup).

9. HAMMA HAMMA - Provides some good fishing for feeding and maturing chinook from late spring through summer during the early morning hours. Access: See 8; hoist and rental boats at Beacon Point Resort (near Mason-Jefferson County line).

BOTTOM FISH

Copper rockfish dominate bottom fish catches from the rock strewn depths of Hood Canal. Rock sole, surf perch, and lingcod are also taken in fair numbers.

TROUT

Some good cutthroat trout fishing is enjoyed along the shorelines of the canal, particularly near the mouths of the larger creeks. Cutthroat fishing in the lower canal can be good from summer through November. A few Dolly Varden are also taken from the estuary of the Skokomish River.

elliott bay to foulweather bluff and everett

figure 3

SALMON AREAS

1. PORT ORCHARD AND DYES INLET - Provides good late fall to mid-winter fishing for feeding chinook salmon. Access: Boat ramps and hoists at Bremerton and Port Orchard.

2. ELLIOTT BAY - The Washington State salmon sport fishery was essentially born on Elliott Bay. Maturing chinook and coho are taken from August through October. These fish are usually abundant throughout the Duwamish estuary (west waterway) during this period. From November through January, feeding chinook are usually abundant. Early morning fishing is best. Access: Ramp, hoist and rental boats on west side of bay; hoists on Duwamish Waterway; ramp on east side of waterway at 1st Avenue South.

3. SKIFF POINT - Produces feeding chinook from late fall through mid-winter. Access: Ramp at Fay Bainbridge State Park; see 1, 2, 4.

4. SHILSHOLE BAY - Fishing season and types of salmon available closely corresponds to Elliott Bay. Access: Ramps, hoists, and rental boats on Shilshole Bay.

5. POINT MONROE - Yields feeding chinook from late fall through mid-winter. Access: ramps at Poulsbo, Suquamish; see 3, 4.

6. AGATE PASSAGE - Some large feeding chinook available from late February through March when herring are spawning in the area. Access: See 3, 4, 5.

7. JEFFERSON HEAD - An important year round fishing area for feeding and maturing chinook. Also yields some coho during the late spring and summer months. Access: See 3, 4, 5.

8. "THE TREES" - A productive late fall through early spring fishing area for feeding chinook. Also yields some maturing chinook during summer months. This area is marked by several evenly spaced poplar trees along the shoreline. Access: See 3, 4; hoists, rental boats at Edmonds.

9/10. POINT WELLS TO EDMONDS - Feeding chinook are taken over the dropoffs at the oil docks during the winter months. Access: See 4, 8.

11. POSSESSION POINT TO SCATCHET HEAD - One of the most popular and productive fishing areas in Washington from May through September for coho, chinook, and pink salmon. This is an early morning fishing area, but the salmon may cooperate later in the day during the late stages of ebb tide. Small chinook are abundant from

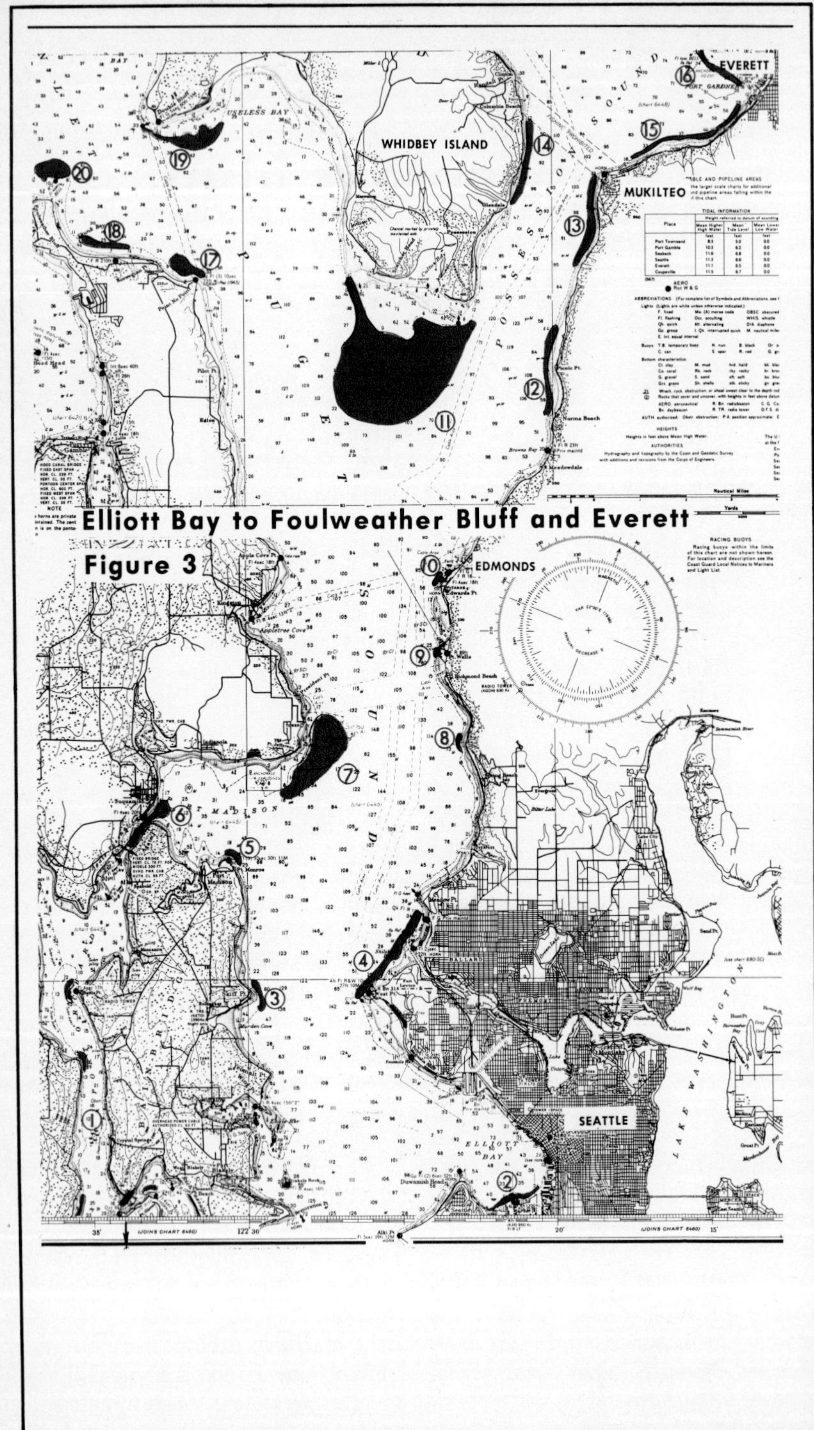
Elliott Bay to Foulweather Bluff and Everett
Figure 3
WHIDBEY ISLAND
EVERETT
MUKILTEO
EDMONDS
SEATTLE

late winter through June; resident coho from late April through August, and ocean coho in September and October. Drift mooching and trolling are both productive techniques. Access: See 8, 9; rental boats at Meadowdale; ramp, hoists and rental boats at Mukilteo.

12/13. MEADOWDALE TO MUKILTEO - Provides good pink salmon fishing from August to mid-September and coho in September and October. Early morning trolling is generally best. Access: See 11.

14. GLENDALE TO COLUMBIA BEACH - Yields good catches of coho, pink, and chinook salmon to trollers from August through October. Access: See 11; ramps, hoists and rental boats at Everett, Columbia Beach, and Glendale.

15. PORT GARDNER - Feeding chinook are taken during the late fall and winter months. Access: See 14.

16. EVERETT - Maturing chinook, coho, and pink salmon are taken by trollers from mid-summer through early fall. Access: See 14; ramps hoists and rental boats on Tulalip Bay.

17. POINT NO POINT - One of the most consistent year round fishing areas on the Sound. Feeding chinook are taken the year round as well as large maturing fish during the summer months. Coho fishing may also be good in September and October. Most good fishermen drift mooch the point during ebb tides. Access: See 11; hoists, rental boats at Hansville.

18. SKUNK BAY - Provides chinook during the winter and spring months. Access: See 17; ramp and hoist near Foulweather Bluff.

19. DOUBLE BLUFF - Once very popular during the spring and summer months for feeding coho and chinook. Although not nearly as dependable in recent years, it still produces during the ebb tides. Access: See 17; hoists, rental boats on Mutiny Bay.

20. FOULWEATHER BLUFF - Feeding chinook and coho are taken from the tide rips north of the bluff during spring and summer. Access: See 18.

BOTTOMFISH

Copper rockfish are the most common bottom fish utilized by anglers in this region followed by Pacific sanddabs, a variety of flounders (including many rock sole and starry flounders), sablefish, and Pacific cod. Sablefish may be especially abundant in the vicinity of Possession Bar during the summer months. Pile perch and striped seaperch are abundant near most of the piers in the area and wherever there are flourishing growths of mussels and barnacles. The artificial breakwaters at Shilshole Bay, Edmonds, and Kingston provide good habitat for copper rockfish, black rockfish, kelp greenling, and lingcod. The Edmonds breakwater is accessible to the shore-bound angler.

TROUT

Some cutthroat trout are taken in the region. The most popular shoreline appears to be the points and creek mouths between Edmonds and Mukilteo.

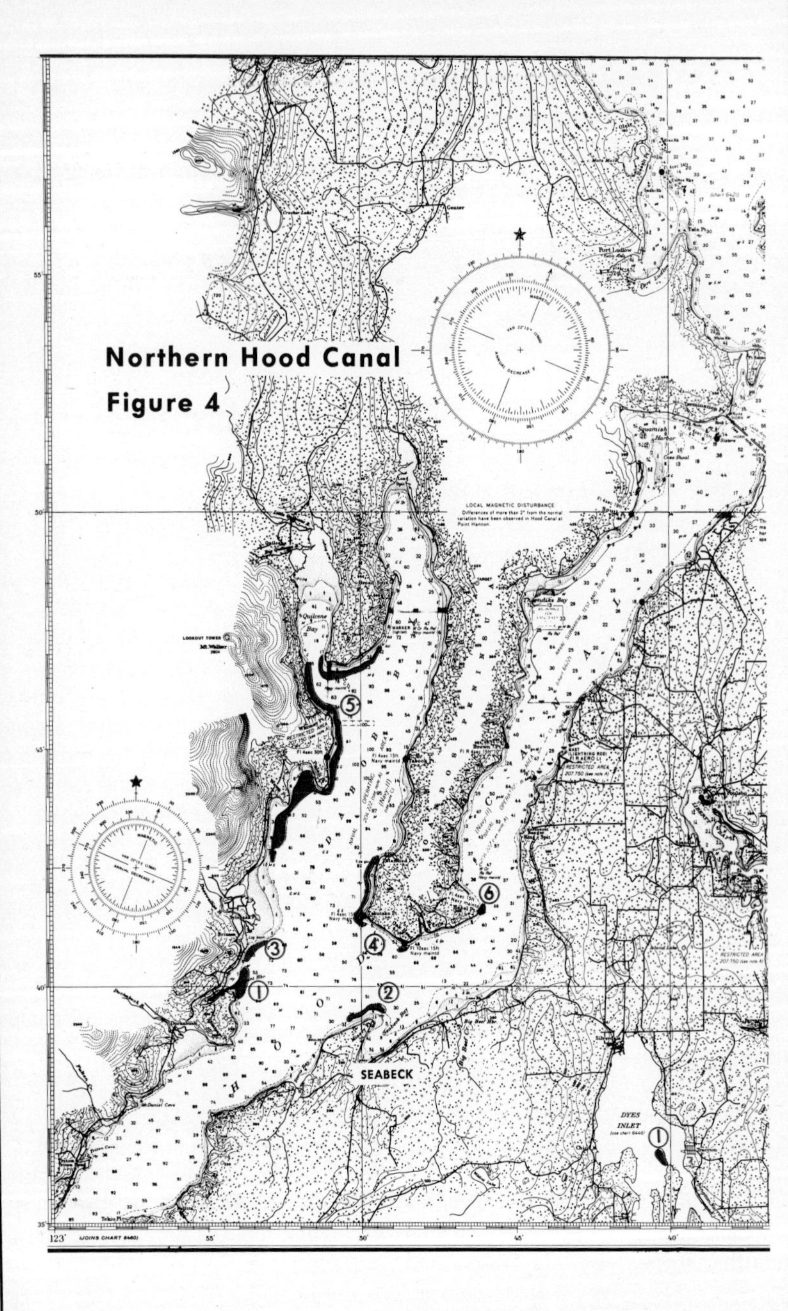
Northern Hood Canal
Figure 4
SEABECK
LOCAL MAGNETIC DISTURBANCE
DYES
INLET
LOOKOUT TOWER
Quilcene
Bay
Port Ludlow
Squamish
Harbor
Thorndyke Bay

northern hood canal

figure 4

SALMON AREAS

1. PLEASANT HARBOR - Can be good for feeding chinook from late winter through early spring. Chinook are frequently taken within the confines of this small, lake-like harbor. Access: Ramp at Quilcene; ramp, hoist, rental boats at Seabeck.

2. MISERY POINT - Feeding chinook from spring through summer. The tide rips between Misery Point and Oak Head usually provide good fishing for feeding coho from late spring through summer and for large ocean run coho during the early fall. Access: See 1.

3. DOSEWALLIPS - Provides some good fishing for pink salmon from August through early September. Access: See 1.

4. TSKUTSKO ("JAPANESE") POINT TO OAK HEAD - May be good for feeding chinook from late winter through summer. The offshore tide rips yield coho from late spring through summer. Access: See 1.

5. DABOB BAY - Usually good for feeding chinook from January through early March. Access: See 1.

6. HAZEL POINT - A popular mid-spring through early summer fishing area for feeding and maturing chinook. Early mornings are best. Access: See 1.

BOTTOM FISH

Copper rockfish, rock sole, and lingcod are the most heavily utilized bottom fish in Northern Hood Canal. Striped seaperch and pile perch are also abundant over suitable habitat.

TROUT

Cutthroat trout are available from summer through early fall in the region. Upper Dabob Bay deserves special mention.

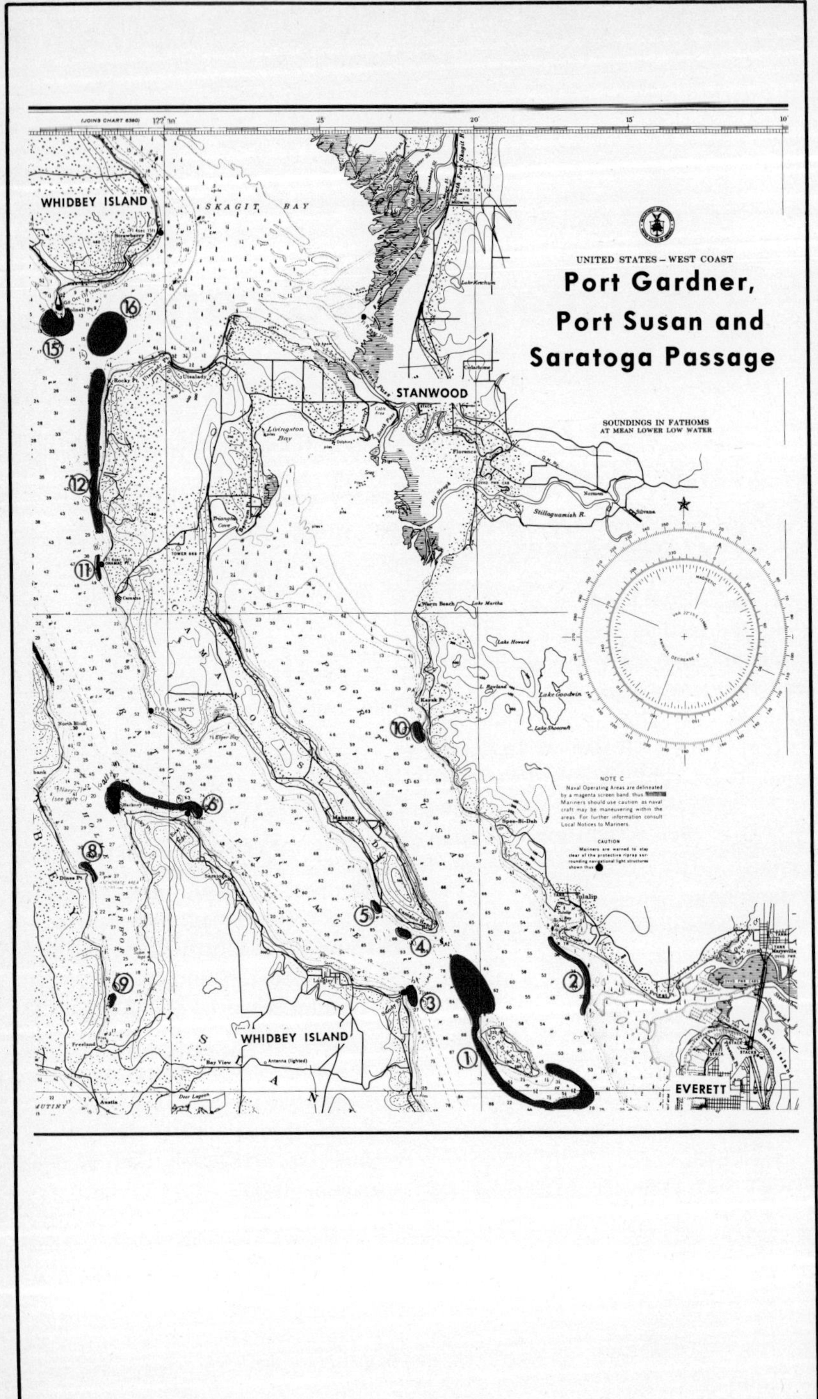

UNITED STATES – WEST COAST
Port Gardner, Port Susan and Saratoga Passage
SOUNDINGS IN FATHOMS AT MEAN LOWER LOW WATER
WHIDBEY ISLAND
SKAGIT BAY
STANWOOD
Livingston Bay
Stillaguamish R.
EVERETT
Tulalip
Smith Island
NOTE C
Naval Operating Areas are delineated by a magenta screen band, thus. Mariners should use caution as naval craft may be maneuvering within the areas. For further information consult Local Notices to Mariners.
CAUTION
Mariners are warned to stay clear of the protective riprap surrounding navigational light structures shown thus
1
2
3
4
5
6
8
9
10
11
12
15
16

port gardner, port susan and saratoga passage

figure 5

SALMON AREAS

1. GEDNEY (HAT) ISLAND - Heavily fished during the summer months for feeding and maturing chinook, resident and ocean-run coho, and pink salmon. The most consistent coho fishing appears to be off the north end of the island. Access: ramps, hoists, and rental boats at Mukilteo, Columbia Beach, Everett, and Tulalip Bay.

2. MISSION BAR - Yields maturing chinook, coho, and pink salmon from mid-summer through fall. This area, from the mouth of the Snohomish River to Gedney Island, was considered a Mecca for salmon anglers through the 1930's. Access: See 1.

3. SANDY POINT - Feeding chinook are taken during the spring and summer months. Access: See 1; ramp, hoist at Langley.

4/5. "PEBBLE BEACH", COXES SPIT - Both spots produce feeding chinook, especially during the winter months. Access: See 3.

6. EAST POINT ("FOX'S SPIT") Offers year round fishing for feeding chinook. Access: ramps, hoists on west shore of Camano Island, ramp on Holmes Harbor.

7. BABY ISLAND - A fine, year round spot for feeding chinook and coho. Salmon are taken up into the very shallow water near the small island. Access: See 1, 6.

8. DINES POINT - Named after a sportsman who pioneered at some of the traditional mooching techniques. Attracts feeding chinook from early winter through early spring. Access: 1, 6.

9. "THE HERRING TRAP" - Spawning herring are trapped in late February and March, but first allowed to spawn on brush placed in the trap for this purpose. Feeding salmon are attracted to the perimeter of the trap where they are taken by anglers using live herring bait without weight. Access: See 1, 6.

10. McKEE BEACH - Once a popular site for feeding chinook from winter through early spring. Access: See 1.

11/12. ONAMAC POINT, NORTH CAMANO - Both spots yield feeding and an occasional maturing chinook or coho from spring to early fall. Can be very good when baitfish are abundant. Access: Ramp, hoists on west shore of Camano Island; ramps on Penn Cove.

13/14. SNATELUM POINT, FORBES POINT - Both spots attract winter blackmouth fishermen. Access: See 11.

15. POLNELL POINT - Occasionally provides good fishing for feeding and maturing chinook during the spring and summer months. Access: See 11.

16. ROCKY POINT - Resident

coho and small chinook are taken here during the spring months. Access: See 11.

BOTTOM FISH

Copper and quillback rockfish, rock sole, English sole, starry flounder, sand sole, sablefish, walleye pollock, and Pacific hake are the principle bottom fish taken by anglers in the area. During the evening and early morning hours hake can be abundant near the surface. The predominantly smooth bottom and absence of large rocks and reefs throughout the region make it unsuitable for many of the more desirable species.

TROUT

Some fine cutthroat trout fishing is available along the shores of Port Susan and Skagit Bay. The shoreline between Tulalip Bay and Kayak Point is noteworthy as is the north shore of Camano Island. Sea-run Dolly Varden reach peak condition in April, earlier than cutthroat, and are taken along the shoreline north of Tulalip and in the vicinity of Skagit Bay.

---

mutiny bay to smith and protection is.

figure 6

SALMON AREAS

1. OAK BAY - Offers feeding chinook from late fall through early spring, and maturing fish from late July through August. Access: Ramps at Port Townsend, Marrowstone Island, Mats Mats; hoists at Port Townsend.

2. "WINDMILL HOLE" - A productive spot for feeding chinook during the winter months and again in late spring and summer. During the latter period, the fish bite well during the last hour or two of daylight. Drift-mooching with sand lance ("Candlefish") bait is a popular method here. Access: hoists, rental boats at Mutiny Bay, Bush Point.

3. LIPLIP POINT - Fished during the summer months for feeding and maturing chinook. Access: See 1.

4. BUSH POINT - A versatile salmon fishing area. The best pink salmon fishing in Puget Sound occurs here from August through early September. Resident coho have been scarce in recent years but ocean run fish are taken from late August through early October. Feeding chinook are available the year round along with some maturing fish in August. Access: See 2.

5. LAGOON POINT - Good fishing for pink salmon from August through early September and ocean-run coho from late August through early October. Access: See 2.

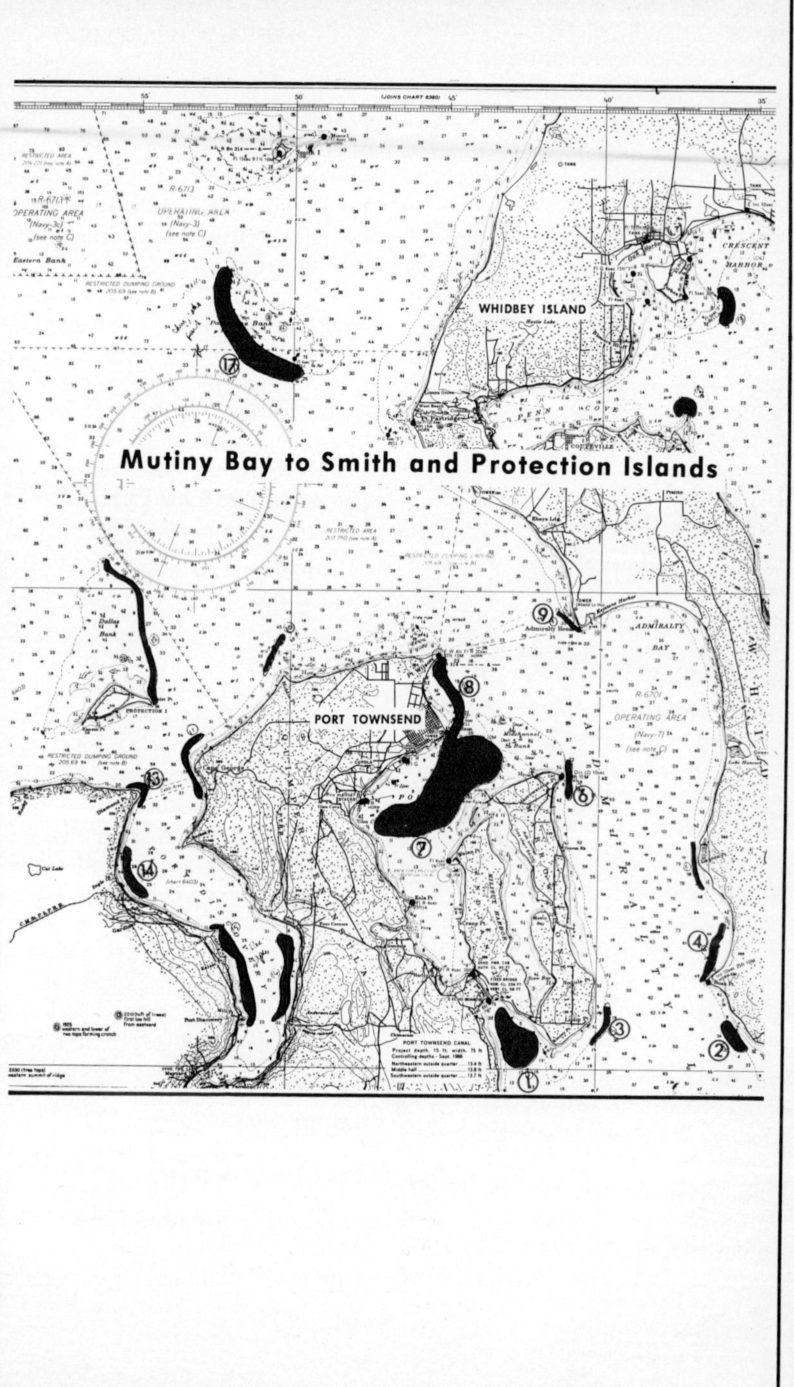
Mutiny Bay to Smith and Protection Islands
WHIDBEY ISLAND
PORT TOWNSEND
ADMIRALTY BAY
CRESCENT HARBOR
PENN COVE
COUPEVILLE
Smith I
Dallas Bank
PROTECTION I
Eastern Bank
R-6713
OPERATING AREA
(Navy-3)
(see note C)
R-6701
OPERATING AREA
(Navy-7)
(see note C)
RESTRICTED DUMPING GROUND
205.69 (see note B)
PORT TOWNSEND CANAL

6. MARROWSTONE POINT - Feeding and maturing chinook during the summer months and some ocean coho in September. Access: See 1.

7. PORT TOWNSEND - The protected waters of the bay yield good catches of feeding chinook during the winter months. Access: See 1.

8. POINT WILSON - Maturing and feeding chinook are taken during the summer months. Pink salmon are available during August and early September and ocean-run coho make an appearance from late August through early October. Access: See 1.

9. ADMIRALTY HEAD - The turbulent waters off the head yield husky chinook to drift moochers during the winter months. Some feeding chinook are available at other times, along with pink salmon in August and early September and ocean coho from late August through early October. Access: Ramp at Keystone.

10. MIDDLE POINT - Maturing chinook and pink salmon from late July through early September. Access: See 1.

11. CAPE GEORGE - Maturing chinook and pink salmon from late July through early September. Access: See 1; ramps, rental boats on Discovery Bay.

12. DALLAS BANK - Maturing chinook from late July through early September, coho from late August through early October, and pink salmon in August and early September. Access: See 11.

13. DIAMOND POINT - A popular summer through early fall spot for maturing chinook, coho, and pinks. Access: See 11.

14/15/16. DISCOVERY BAY - Provides relatively pleasant and productive fishing for feeding chinook from November through March. The lack of current usually excludes drifting as a method of fishing here. Access: See 11.

17. PARTRIDGE BANK - Provides good fishing for feeding and maturing chinook, coho and pink salmon from January through October. Access: See 1; ramps at Keystone, west shore of Whidbey Island opposite Oak Harbor, and Deception Pass State Park.

BOTTOM FISH

Although there is some good angling for bottom fish on the inner Sound, the great fishing begins here along the eastern fringes of Juan de Fuca Strait. The many rocks, reefs, kelp beds, and tidal currents provide ideal habitat for lingcod, kelp greenling, and a variety of rockfishes. Black, copper, quillback, and canary rockfish are some of the more common species. Some Pacific halibut are also taken from the sandy banks and they are specifically sought during the late winter months at Admiralty Head.

On Admiralty Inlet, the fishing opportunities are much like those described for the region from Elliott Bay to Foulweather Bluff and Everett.

TROUT

A unique steelhead fishery occurs during the winter months from the beaches of Bush and Lagoon points.

north whidbey island to the canadian border

figure 7

SALMON AREAS

1. WEST BEACH AND DECEPTION PASS - Large maturing chinook, bound for the Skagit and Fraser Rivers, congregate in the shallows off West Beach from July through early August. These fish often occur in depths of less than 10 feet. Fair numbers of pink and coho salmon are taken in the deeper water throughout the area. "The Hole" located just west of the Deception Pass bridge near the Whidbey Island shore is heavily fished for large maturing chinook. The popular method here is to use a motor to hold in the eddy that forms during the ebb tide and fish a short line with a herring bait. Many of these large fish are bound for the Skagit River. Access: Ramps in Deception Pass State Park; ramp, hoists on Coronet Bay; hoist at La Conner; hoist, rental boats on Skagit Bay.

2. HOPE ISLAND - The east end of the island fished during the flood tide, and the west end fished on the ebb, are well known for trophy sized chinook. In the mid-1940's, upwards of 1,000 salmon a year, averaging 28 lbs. each, were taken here but since then, the catch has declined considerably. Far more Skagit River chinook are now taken from Deception Pass and the river itself than were taken at Hope Island during these peak years. Hope Island fishing is a genuine specialty with almost all of the chinook being taken by trolling large spoons and plugs, along a precise course. The season extends from May through early August. Access: See 1.

3. LANGLEY ("BIZ") POINT - Feeding chinook during the winter and spring months. Access: See 1; ramps, hoists on Fidalgo Island.

4. ICEBERG POINT - Fished during the spring and summer months for chinook. Access: See 1, 3.

5. LOPEZ PASS - The relatively protected confines of the pass yield husky feeding chinook during the winter months. Access: See 1, 3.

6. REEF POINT - Fished during the spring, summer, and early fall for chinook and coho salmon. Access: See 1, 3.

7/8. GUEMES CHANNEL - Popular with local anglers for winter chinook. Access: See 1, 3.

9. STRAWBERRY ISLAND, TIDE POINT, TOWHEAD ISLAND - Fished year round for feeding chinook. Some maturing chinook are taken during the summer months with ocean coho making an appearance from late August through early October. Access: See 1, 3.

10/11. JACK ISLAND AND WILLIAM POINT - Both yield

feeding chinook from winter through early spring. Access: See 1, 3.

12. EAST SOUND - The sound, particularly near its entrance, is usually good for feeding chinook throughout the winter months. Access: See 1, 3; hoists, ramps, rental boats on Orcas Island; ramp on Blakely Island.

13. POINT LAWRENCE - A well-known late spring through early fall spot for feeding and maturing chinook and coho. Access: See 12; ramps at Bellingham, Lummi Island; hoists at Gooseberry Point on Lummi Island.

14. SINCLAIR ISLAND - Fished during the spring and summer months for feeding chinook. Access: See 13.

15. LUMMI ROCKS - Yields chinook and coho during the summer months. Access: See 13.

16/17. HALE PASSAGE - Some husky feeding chinook are taken here during winter. Access: See 13.

18. NORTHEAST SHORE OF ORCAS ISLAND - Trollers work the shoreline during the summer months for feeding, as well as maturing, chinook. Access: See 13.

19. WALDRON ISLAND - Fished from July through September for feeding and maturing coho. Pinks are also available during August. The south shore of Skipjack Island yields some maturing chinook in July and August. Access: See 13.

20. MOSQUITO PASS - Some large feeding chinook are taken from the shallow confines of the pass from winter through early spring. Ocean coho make an appearance in the deeper waters off the south end of the pass in September. Access: Ramps, hoists, rental boats on San Juan Island.

21. SPIEDEN CHANŇEL - Good fishing for large feeding chinook

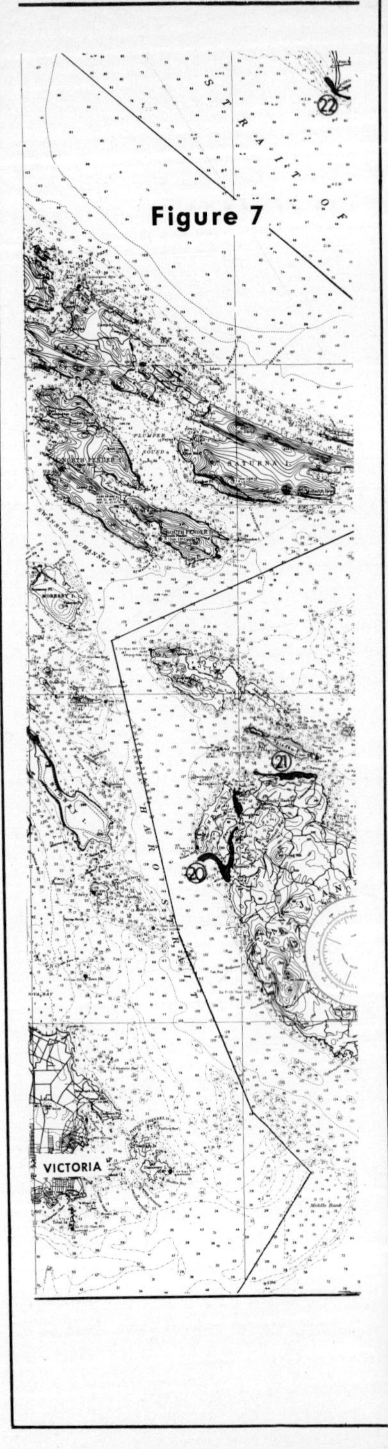

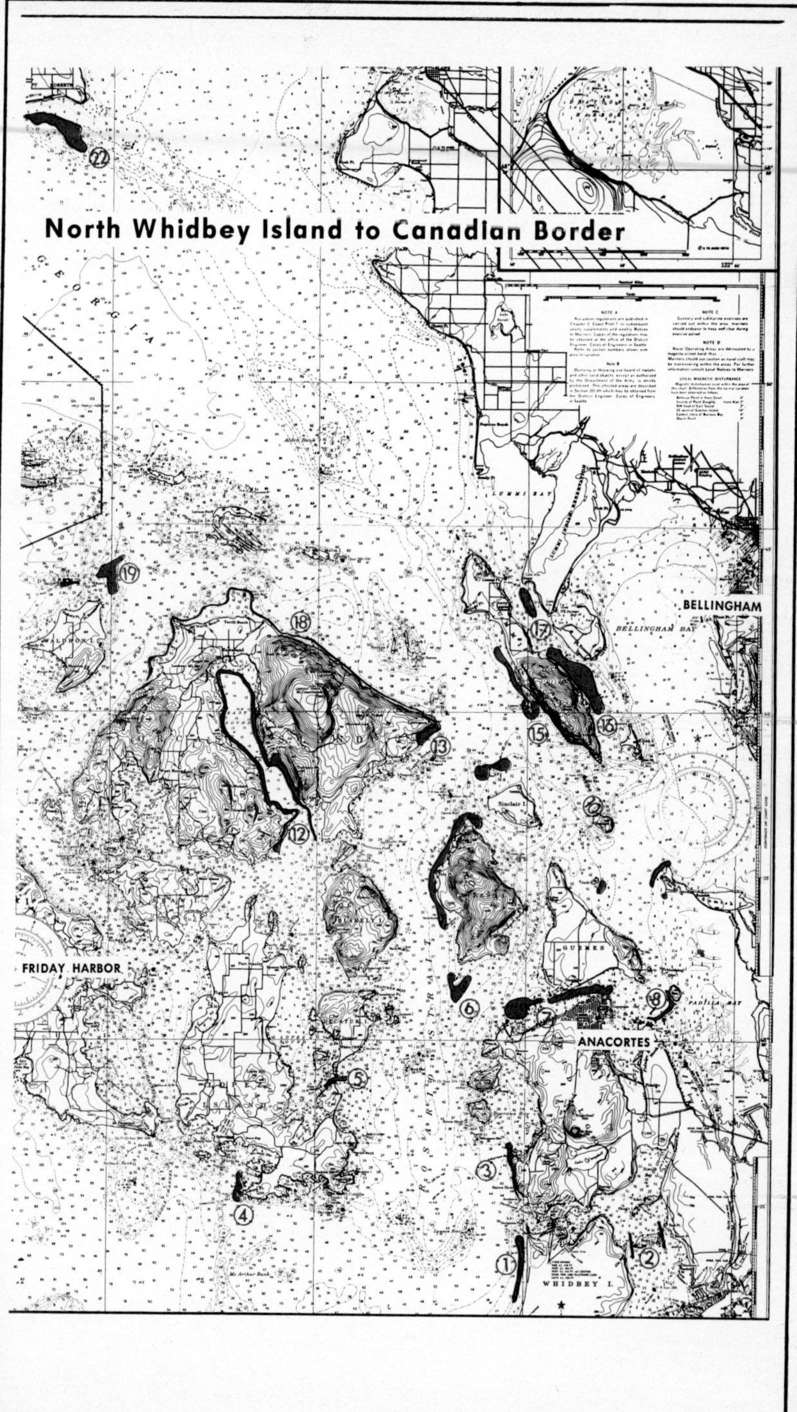
North Whidbey Island to Canadian Border
BELLINGHAM
BELLINGHAM BAY
LUMMI BAY
Sinclair I.
FRIDAY HARBOR
ANACORTES
PADILLA BAY
WHIDBEY I.
22
19
18
17
16
15
13
12
10
8
7
6
5
4
3
2
1

throughout winter months. Access: See 20.

22. POINT ROBERTS - Heavily fished by Canadian anglers during summer months for feeding and maturing chinook and coho. Pink salmon are available in August and early September. Access: Ramps, hoists at Blaine and Birch Bay; ramp at Point Roberts.

BOTTOM FISH

The steep, rocky vermicular shorelines of the islands, the offshore rocks, reefs, shoals, and tidal currents provide ideal habitat for lingcod, kelp greenling and a variety of rockfish. Of the latter, copper, quillback, black, rasphead, and canary are most common. Pacific cod are also abundant from late winter through early spring over the sand, gravel, and mud bottoms occuring in the area. West Beach, Bellingham Bay, and Georgia Strait yield large numbers of these fish to commercial trawlers fishing the depths greater than 90 feet.

TROUT

The lower estuaries of the Skagit River around the Bald, Ika, and Goat Islands, the Swinomish Channel, and the beaches in the vicinity of Hope Island offer the finest fishing for sea-run Dolly Varden available in Washington. This fishing peaks in April and May. Although trolling in the estuaries is the most common fishing method, they can be taken from the shores of Swinomish Channel around low tide and from the Fidalgo Island beaches near Hope Island at high tide.

Cutthroat are also taken in these same areas throughout the late spring and summer months. The South Fork of the Skagit (the southern portion of the estuary) is good for both cutthroat and Dollies.

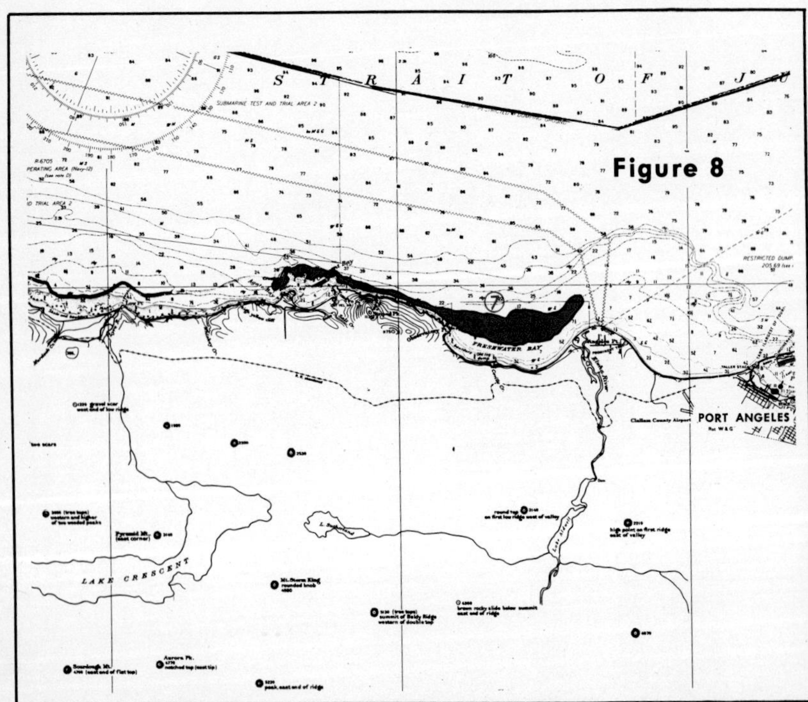

Figure 8

east juan de fuca strait

figure 8

SALMON AREAS

1. SEQUIM BAY – Feeding chinook are taken from the confines of the bay during the winter months. Access: Ramps and rental boats in Sequim Bay.

2. DUNGENESS BAY – Maturing spring chinook, bound for the Dungeness River are caught in late April and May. Access: Ramp on Dungeness Bay.

3. DUNGENESS SPIT – Fished during the summer months for feeding and maturing chinook. Pinks are available from late July through early September. Ocean coho usually are available from late August through early October. Access: See 2.

4. GREEN POINT – Feeding chinook are taken the year round in this versatile area along with maturing fish from July through early September. Pink salmon show from August through early September and some ocean coho are taken from late August through early October. Access: See 2; ramp on Ediz Hook; hoists, rental boats on Ediz Hook and Port Angeles Harbor.

5. PORT ANGELES (Harbor) –

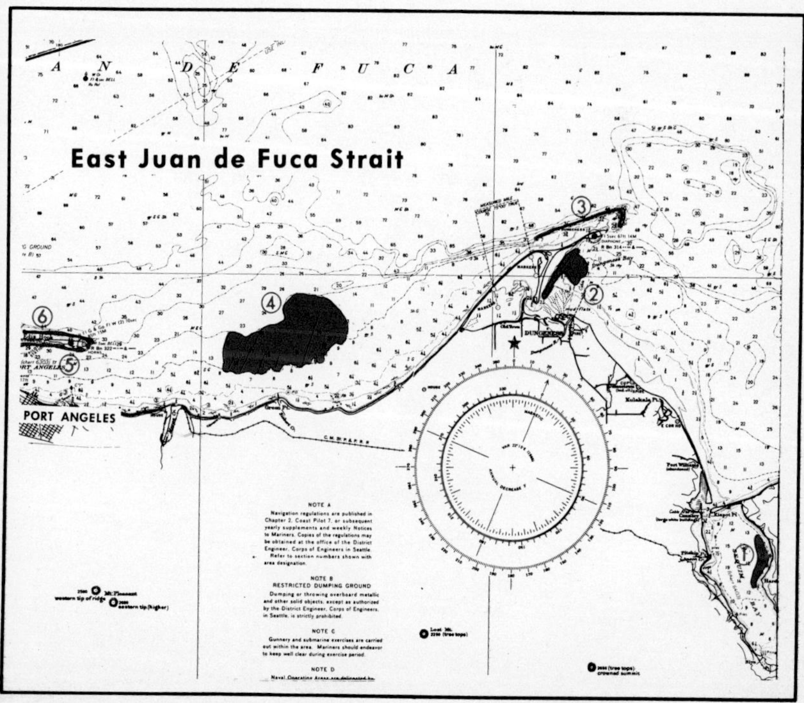

Some large feeding chinook are taken close in along the inside of spit during the winter months. Access: See 4.

6. EDIZ HOOK – Fished during the summer months for feeding and maturing chinook. Can be a fine spot for large chinook from June through early September. Usually an early morning bite. Coho and pink salmon are usually taken in the off-shore rips in August and September. Access: See 4.

7. FRESHWATER BAY TO AGATE BAY – Popular from late winter through summer for feeding and maturing chinook. Pink salmon are available in August and early September. Look for coho from August through September in the off-shore rips. Access: See 4; ramp on Freshwater Bay; hoist, rental boats on Crescent Bay.

Bottom Fish

In much of the eastern portion of this region, rocks and reefs are scarce and one must first find them to do well on lingcod and rockfish. Extensive sand and gravel shoals are, however, home for a variety of flounders including halibut. In late winter and early spring, Pacific cod may be abundant in depths greater than 20 fathoms.

A major part of our halibut sport catch occurs in this region. Some of the more popular fishing locations for halibut are off Dungeness Spit, Green Point, and Crescent Bay. The latter area is also one of Washington's most popular fishing areas for a variety of rockfishes (including copper, black, canary, and quillback), lingcod, and kelp greenling.

... this is what it's

all about!!

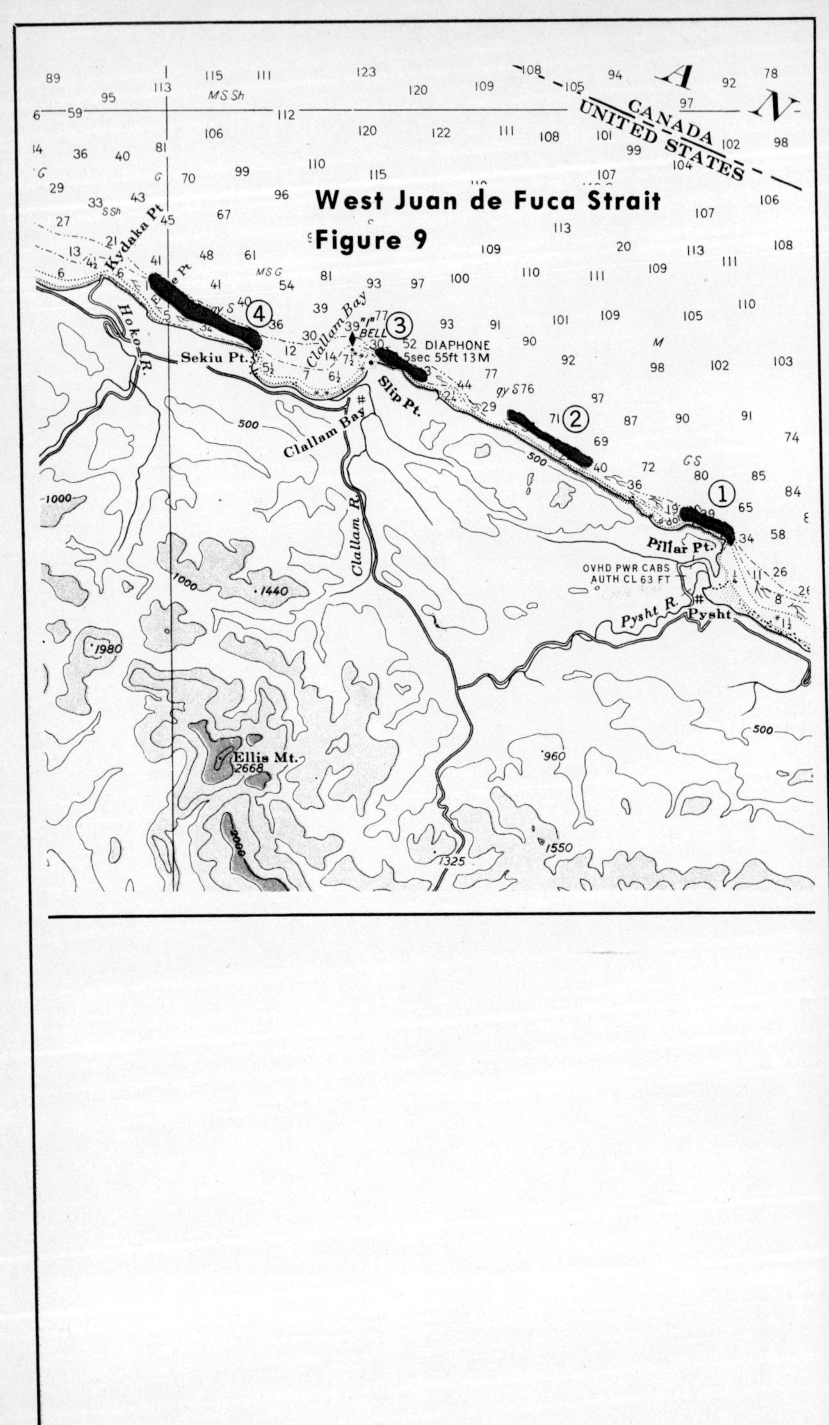
West Juan de Fuca Strait
Figure 9
CANADA
UNITED STATES
Kydaka Pt
Hoko R.
Sekiu Pt.
Clallam Bay
BELL
DIAPHONE
5sec 55ft 13M
Slip Pt.
Clallam Bay
Clallam R.
Pillar Pt.
OVHD PWR CABS
AUTH CL 63 FT
Pysht R.
Pysht
Ellis Mt.
2668
1440
1980
960
1550
1325

west juan de fuca strait

figure 9

SALMON AREAS

1. PILLAR POINT – One of our finest summer through early fall fishing locations for maturing and feeding chinook. Early morning fishing is generally best. Coho are available in the offshore rips from August through early October. Look for pinks from August through early September. Access: Ramp at Pillar Point; ramp and rental boats at Silver-King Resort; ramps, hoists, rental boats and charters at Sekiu.

2. "THE COAL MINE" – A fine early morning bet in July and August for maturing chinook. Access: See 1.

3. "MUSSOLINI ROCK" – A large rock with a silhouette resembling a seaward gazing dictator marks a fine spot for large maturing chinook. Early mornings in July and August are best. The large fish tend to be just outside of the kelp-line. Access: See 1.

4. SEKIU POINT TO MOUTH OF THE HOKO RIVER – By far the most heavily fished area in the region. Offers consistently good February through late April fishing for medium sized feeding chinook. A bait fished just off bottom in the morning usually produces the best results. An abundance of sand lance (candlefish) appears to attract these feeding chinook. One of our finest areas for large maturing chinook in July and August. Ocean coho usually appear in August and are taken mostly offshore through early October. Pinks are abundant from August through early September when they usually comprise a major portion of the odd-year salmon catch. Access: See 1.

BOTTOM FISH

The shoreline of the western strait is rocky, steep, and lined with kelp. The large populations of black, china, copper, and quillback rockfishes, greenling and lingcod along this coast have hardly been touched.

Ocean-borne swells sweep far into the strait providing suitable habitat for redtail surfperch in a few locations. The beach between East and West Twin Rivers and the crescent of beach at Deep Creek offer fine fishing for both redtails and striped seaperch.

Away from shore, the bottom is quite smooth and a variety of flounders including arrowtooth flounder, rock sole, petrale sole, are fairly abundant. A few hundred Pacific halibut are also taken each year, principally by anglers mooching for salmon.

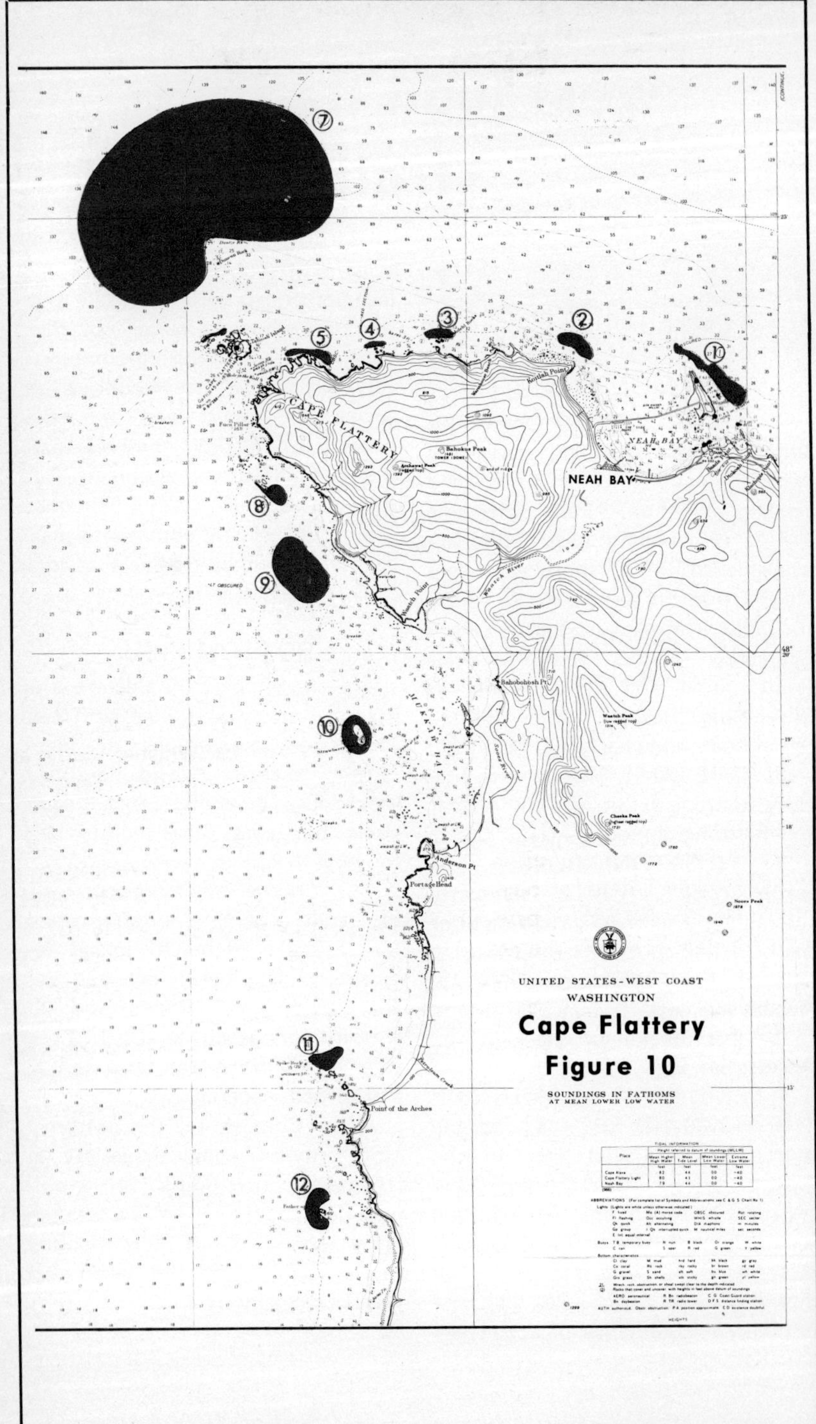
UNITED STATES-WEST COAST
WASHINGTON
Cape Flattery
Figure 10
SOUNDINGS IN FATHOMS
AT MEAN LOWER LOW WATER
CAPE FLATTERY
NEAH BAY
Koitlah Point
Archawat Peak
Bahokus Peak
Waatch Point
Waatch River
Bahobohosh Pt.
MUKKAW BAY
Sooes River
Waatch Peak
Cheeka Peak
Anderson Pt
Portage Head
Point of the Arches
Petroleum Creek
Sooes Peak

cape flattery

figure 10

SALMON AREAS

1. WAADAH ISLAND – Partly because of its accessibility, it is the most popular fishing area in the region. Feeding chinook are available the year round. Large maturing fish are taken from June through early September but fishing for them is best from mid-July through mid-August. Pink salmon are taken from late July through early September. Coho fishing is best inside the strait from August through mid-september. Access: Ramps, hoists, rental and charter boats at Neah Bay.

2. KOITLAH ("Garbage") POINT – Feeding and large maturing chinook from June through early September; best from mid-July through mid-August. Access: See 1.

3. "MIDWAY" ROCKS – Large maturing chinook, as well as some feeders, from June through early September. Again, best from mid-July through mid-August. Fish just outside the kelp at dawn and around tide changes. Access: See 1.

4. "SLANT ROCK" – Same story as Midway. Access: See 1.

5. "MUSHROOM ROCK" – A repeat of Midway and Slant Rocks. Access: See 1.

6. TATOOSH – Another spot for large chinook. Access: See 1.

7. "THE WHISTLE" (Buoy) – Coho and pink salmon are taken over a broad area throughout Juan de Fuca Strait. The area around the Whistle buoy, however, is one of the more precise and consistent fishing locations for coho. Feeding fish are usually found among the area's spectacular tide rips from June through early September. Access: See 1.

8. "SKAGWAY ROCKS" – Good shallow water fishing for chinook. Usually best in July and early August. Access: See 1.

9-10. "GREENBANK", STRAWBERRY ROCK, SPIKE ROCK, FATHER AND SON – All are good bets for chinook in July and early August. Access: See 1.

Bottom fish

The coastline is rocky, spectacular, and teeming with black rockfish, kelp greenling, and lingcod. In deeper water, china, copper, quillback, and rasphead rockfish are abundant. Just southeast of the Whistler buoy at Duncan Rock, yellowtail and black rockfish are so thick that it is difficult to lower a bait a few fathoms without immediately catching a fish. Frequently, these rockfish are feeding at the surface.

For the shore bound angler, the jetty at Neah Bay, extending to Waadah Island, offers fine fishing for black rockfish. A jig worked between the kelp will produce good results. Redtail surfperch can be taken from the sandy beaches of Mukkaw Bay and the lower estuary of Sooes River. There are various places in the vicinity of Neah Bay where jigs can be cast from the rocky shoreline for black rockfish, kelp greenling, and lingcod, but in most cases this is recommended only for the sure-footed and adventurous anglers.

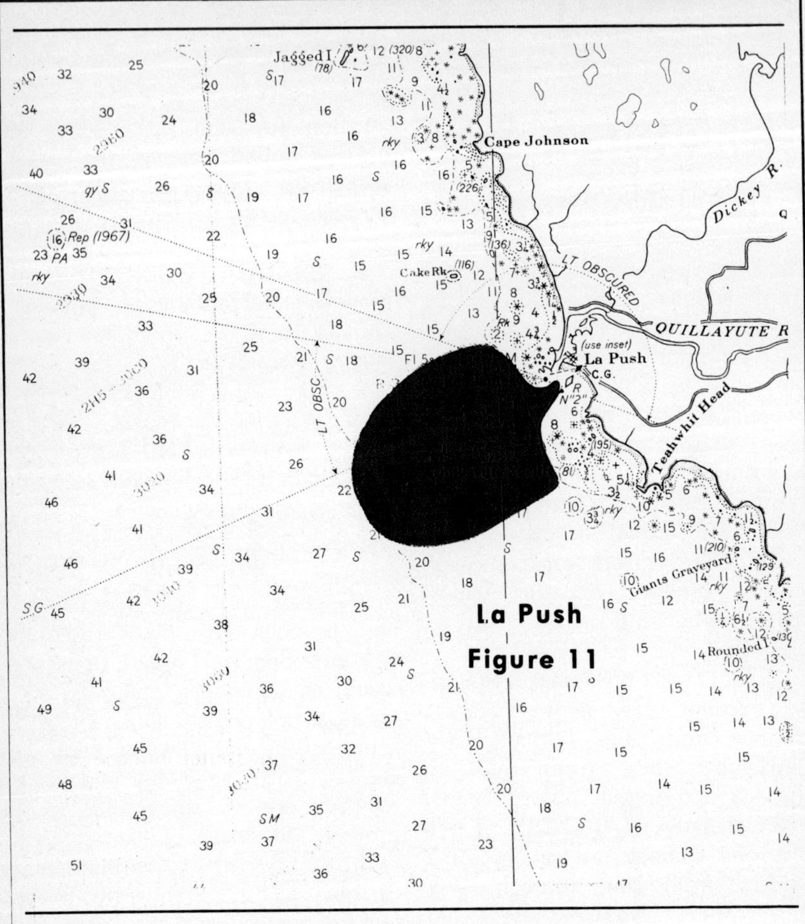

La Push

Figure 11

la push

figure 11

Salmon areas

From July through August, depending upon the variable distribution of feeding salmon, LaPush can provide the best in coho salmon fishing. Most of the fishing occurs over smooth sand within five miles of port. Although most of the chinook landed are rather small, large maturing fish are taken inshore along the spectacular pinnacles and rocks that abound in the region. In addition, large maturing Quillayute chinook are taken at the mouth of the river in September and early October.

Compared to the formidable bars at the entrance to the Columbia River, Willapa Bay and Grays Harbor, passage to and from the open ocean is usually not a problem for the small boat fisherman at LaPush. Charter and rental boats as well as ramps and hoists are available at this picturesque location.

Bottom fish

Black and blue rockfish, lingcod, and greenling are abundant against the surf washed rocks and over the reefs near LaPush. A variety of flounders, including fair numbers of Pacific halibut, are taken off the smooth sand bottom. Salmon anglers may also encounter hungry schools of jack mackerel. The secluded sandy beaches in the area provide ample opportunity for redtail surfperch fishing. Youngsters amuse themselves by the hour catching Pacific tomcod that school around the moorage floats at LaPush during the summer months. There are a number of locations, near LaPush, where the sure-footed angler can clamber onto the rocks and cast a jig to black rockfish, kelp greenling, and lingcod.

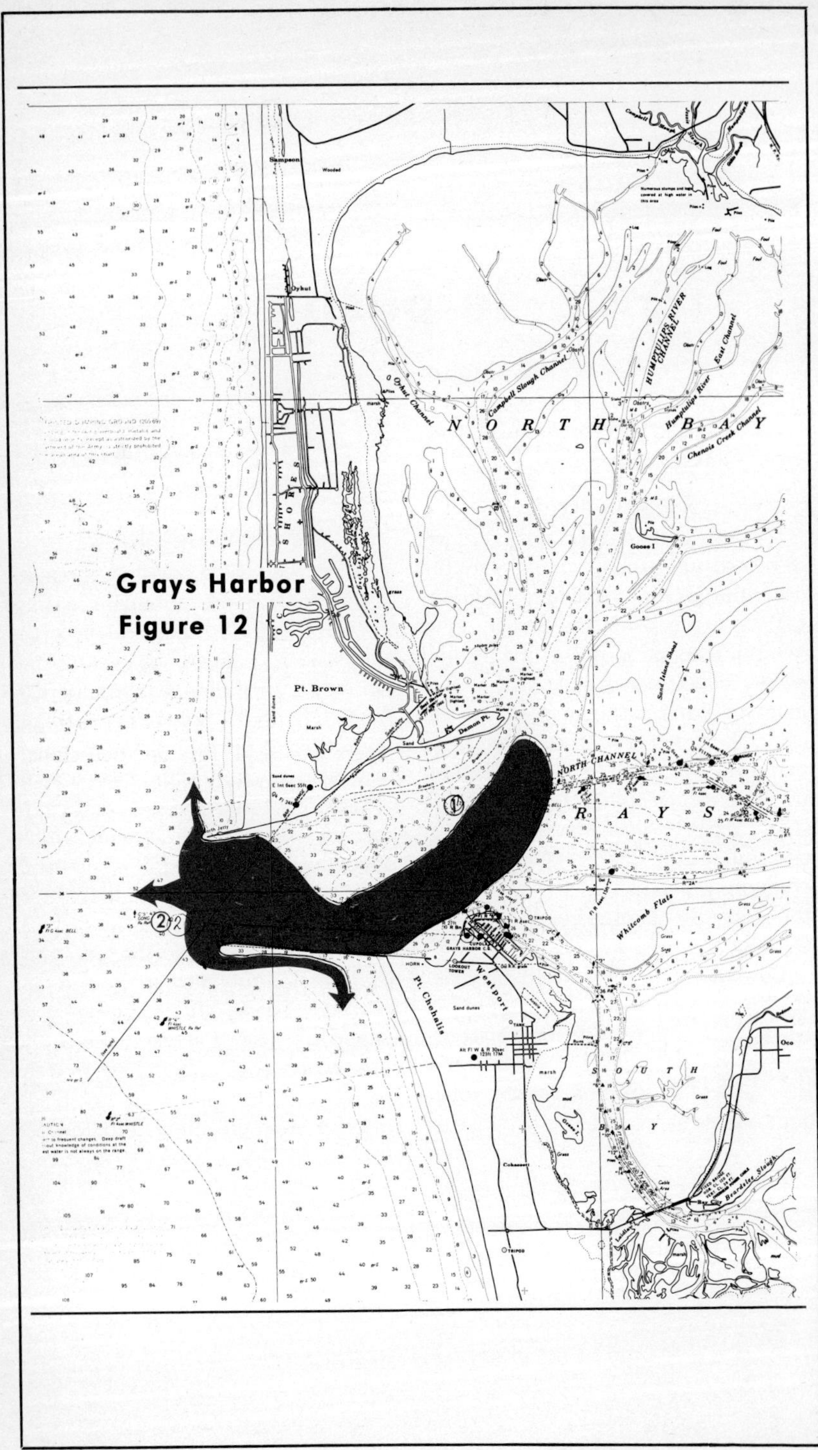
Grays Harbor
Figure 12
NORTH BAY
GRAYS
SOUTH BAY
NORTH CHANNEL
Pt. Brown
Damon Pt.
Pt. Chehalis
Westport
Whitcomb Flats
Sand Island Shoal
Goose I
Campbell Slough Channel
Humptulips River
Chenois Creek Channel
Oyhut Channel
Sampson
Oyhut
Cohassett
Bay City
Beardslee Slough
Sand dunes
marsh

grays harbor

figure 12

SALMON AREAS

Good salmon fishing is available off Grays Harbor from mid-April through mid-October, however, over 90% of the fishing pressure occurs from June through September. Although there are more coho than chinook taken off Grays Harbor, the area yields more and larger chinook than any of Washington's other coastal fishing ports. A large modern charter fleet operates out of Westport and charters are also available across the harbor at Ocean Shores. The town of Westport is primarily a sport fishing center, featuring a public ramp as well as commercial launching facilities. The bar, at the entrance to the harbor, can be treacherous – especially during ebb tides.

Large numbers of coho and chinook are taken each year from the south jetty at Westport. The channel site of the jetty is fished for salmon, with best results from late July through September.

1. From August through early October, some large maturing chinook as well as coho are taken inside the harbor.

2. Most of the sport catch occurs over a broad, featureless area outside of Grays Harbor. In the early season, the boats range up to twenty miles offshore, but as the season progresses, fishing occurs inshore to just outside the surf line. Even late in the season, the larger boats may range far north or south.

BOTTOM FISH

Black rockfish and lingcod are often encountered when fishing along the Grays Harbor jetties or when over one of the few reefs in the region. Starry flounder and sand sole are taken incidentally by salmon anglers as well as an occasional halibut. Pacific hake and jack mackerel are sometimes abundant enough to pester salmon anglers.

For the shore-bound angler, the south jetty at Westport can provide good fishing for redtail surfperch, black rockfish, kelp greenling, and lingcod. The miles of sandy beaches north and south of Grays Harbor provide ample room for surf fishing for redtail. Large numbers of Pacific tomcod are available around moorage floats at Westport and Ocean Shores.

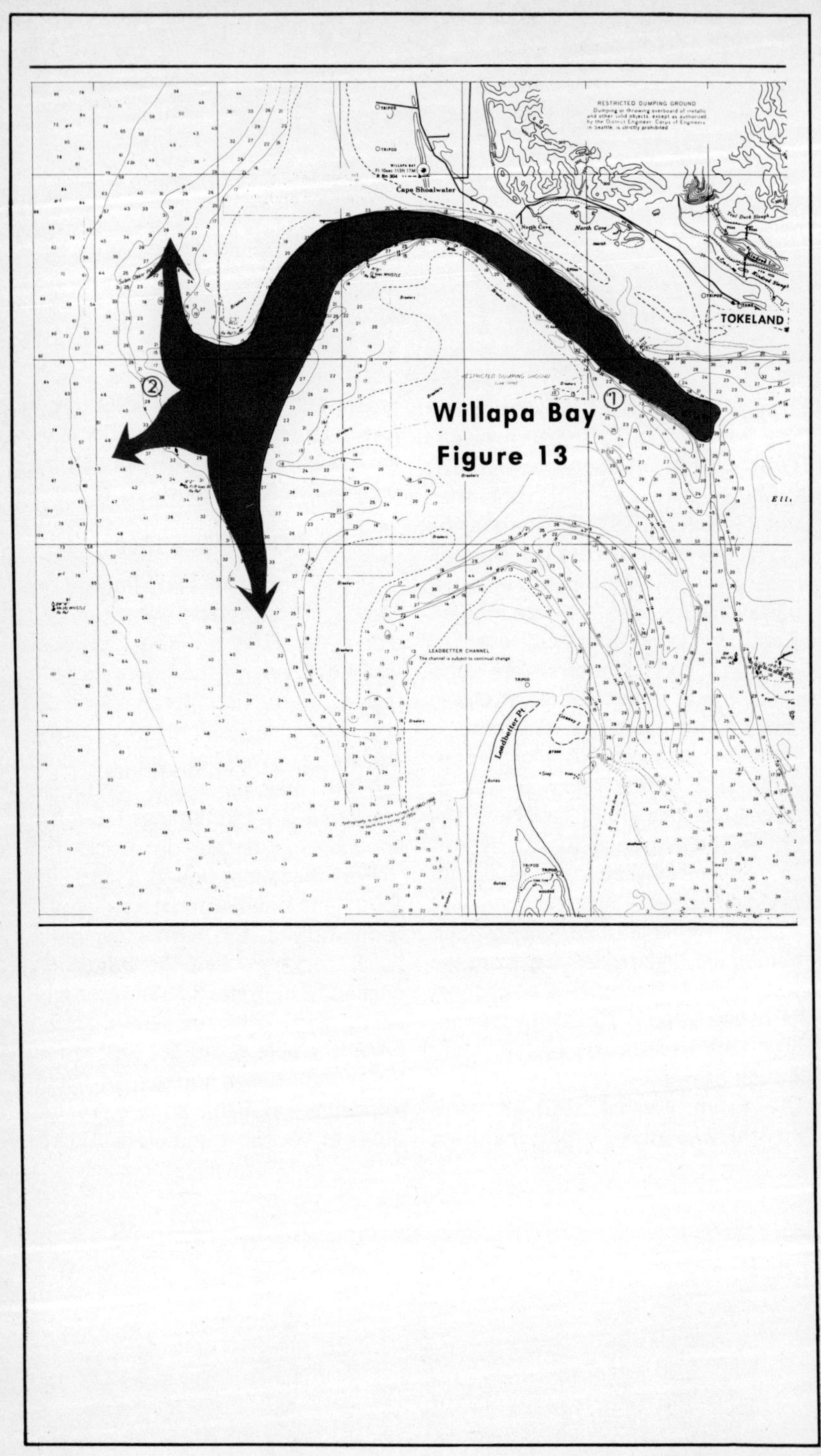

Willapa Bay
Figure 13

willapa bay

figure 13

SALMON AREAS

Salmon fishing around Willapa Bay can be superb, but the unprotected bar at its entrance is treacherous and most of the local fishing effort originates in Grays Harbor.

1. During July and August, excellent chinook salmon fishing is sporadically available within the bay. There is a public boat ramp at Tokeland and reasonable safe small boat fishing can be enjoyed inside the bay during the flood tides.

2. The fishing patterns off Willapa Bay are similar to those off Grays Harbor.

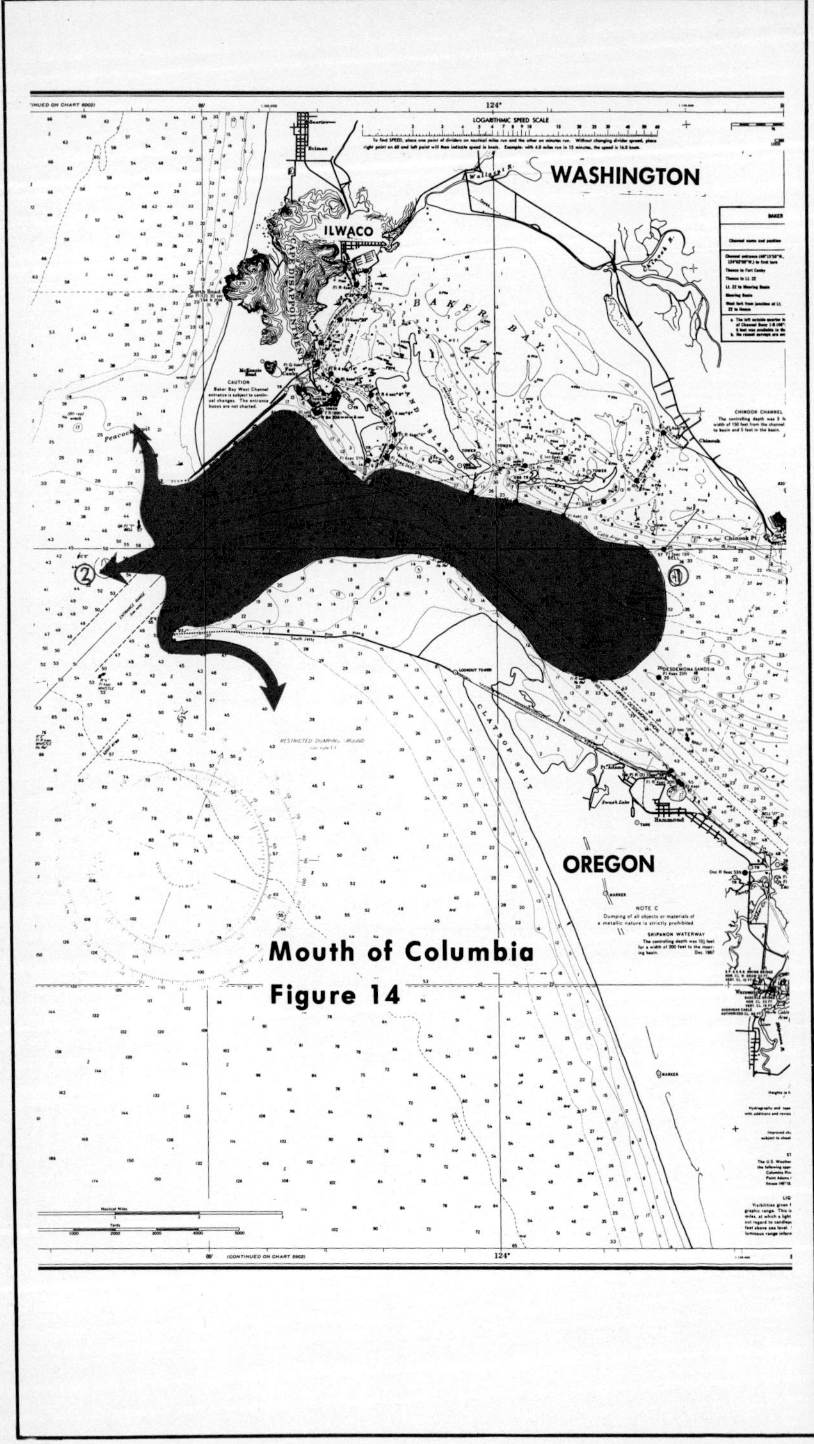

Mouth of Columbia

Figure 14

mouth of the columbia

figure 14

SALMON AREAS

In recent years, due primarily to fine coho fishing and newly developed facilities, this area has become one of the most productive salmon sport fishing regions on the Pacific Coast. Charter boats, pay launching facilities, and public boat ramps are all available at and near Ilwaco. Although many small boats fish off the mouth of the river, conditions on the bar, especially during ebb tides, can be hazardous.

Fishing is usually good throughout the summer, but best in August and early September. Small feeding chinook are abundant, constituting the major portion of the catch, and large maturing chinook bound for the river are taken in good numbers during the last three weeks of August. Many salmon are taken by anglers fishing from the north jetty during August and September.

1. Fished from August through early September for maturing chinook and coho salmon.

2. The major salmon fishing area occurs over a broad expanse of ocean on and outside the Columbia River bar.

BOTTOM FISH

Fishing for other salt-water fish in the region is much like that described off Grays Harbor, except that yellowtail and widow rockfish, rather than black rockfish, are the most common. The Long Beach Peninsula offers miles of beach for redtail surfperch fishing. Black rockfish, redtail surfperch, lingcod, and greenling are taken from the north jetty. Redtails and Pacific tomcod are caught from the "fishing rocks" just north of Cape Disappointment.

filleting, skinning and steaking

by nick pasquale

The following series of illustrations and techniques have been designed to assist salt-water fishermen in preparing their catches of bottomfish for cooking. There is no need for the enjoyment to end when the boat is docked. Continued satisfaction from the fishing trip can be had by sitting down to a meal of really fresh fish. A good many anglers are somewhat awed by the shapes of the various species of bottom fish that they have caught and wonder:

Nick Pasquale

bottomfish, salmon

"Well, we got 'em, now what do we do with 'em?"

Actually, all one needs is patience, practice, and the proper fillet knife to make his catch ready for the skillet.

A typical catch will usually contain both flounders and roundfish, such as rockfish, lingcod, and Pacific cod. The basic filleting techniques will be nearly identical for all flatfish, as will the techniques for filleting roundfish. All bottomfish need not be filleted. Some may be filleted. Some may be dressed and cut into steaks, or some may be prepared to be utilized whole.

equipment

The equipment shown eases the task of preparing the catch for cooking and should include the following:

1. A SMOOTH PIECE OF ¾-INCH PLYWOOD about 15 inches by 36 inches. The size of the board can vary to suit individual needs. One side may be used for dressing and cutting up fish, reserving the smoothest side for filleting fish. A smooth, flat board is a must when cutting the skin from a fillet.

2. A FINE OIL STONE. Under normal use, a good oil stone should last nearly a lifetime. The original investment should be for the best stone available. A Washita stone is an excellent one. A light oil provides a good cutting medium and a dash of lighter fluid with the oil keeps the stone from getting gummy and also gives it more "cut".

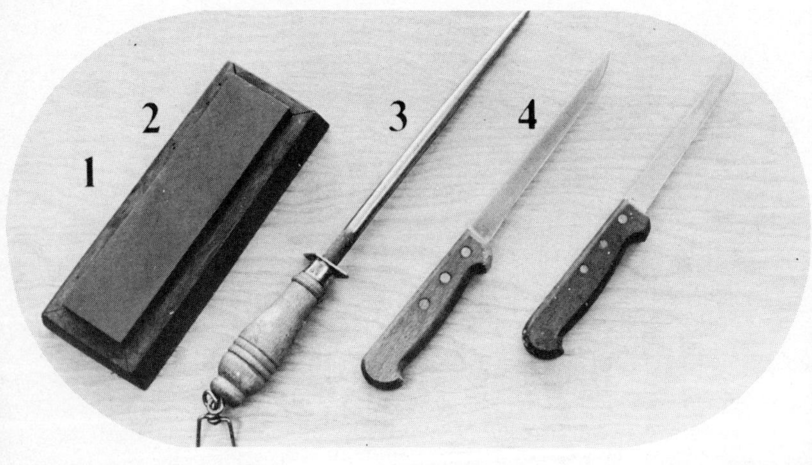

3. A STEEL. A steel is not a knife sharpener but a tool used to "set up" the edge on a knife that has been honed on a stone and should be used sparingly. A couple of light passes of the knife edge on the steel is usually sufficient to restore the cutting edge of the knife.

4. THE KNIVES. One good quality fillet knife and one stiff knife suitable for cutting through the backbone of some fishes are recommended. Here again, the knife should be the best available. For normal sportsman use, a knife should last indefinitely. Good quality, stainless steel knives are available at marine supply stores.

5. A COTTON GLOVE (LEFT HAND). A washable, cotton glove is a most necessary item. Not only does it allow the fish to be held securely but it also protects your hand from the numerous spines present on some truly edible fishes.

preparing flounder

filleting

The most common method of removing the edible portions of a good-size flounder is by filleting. This method yields two boneless fillets of excellent quality.

1. Remove the fillet from the white side first. Grasp the head in the left hand and make a shallow, diagonal cut from behind the head extending just past the mid-line of the fish. This allows the next cut to pass behind the stomach cavity.

1

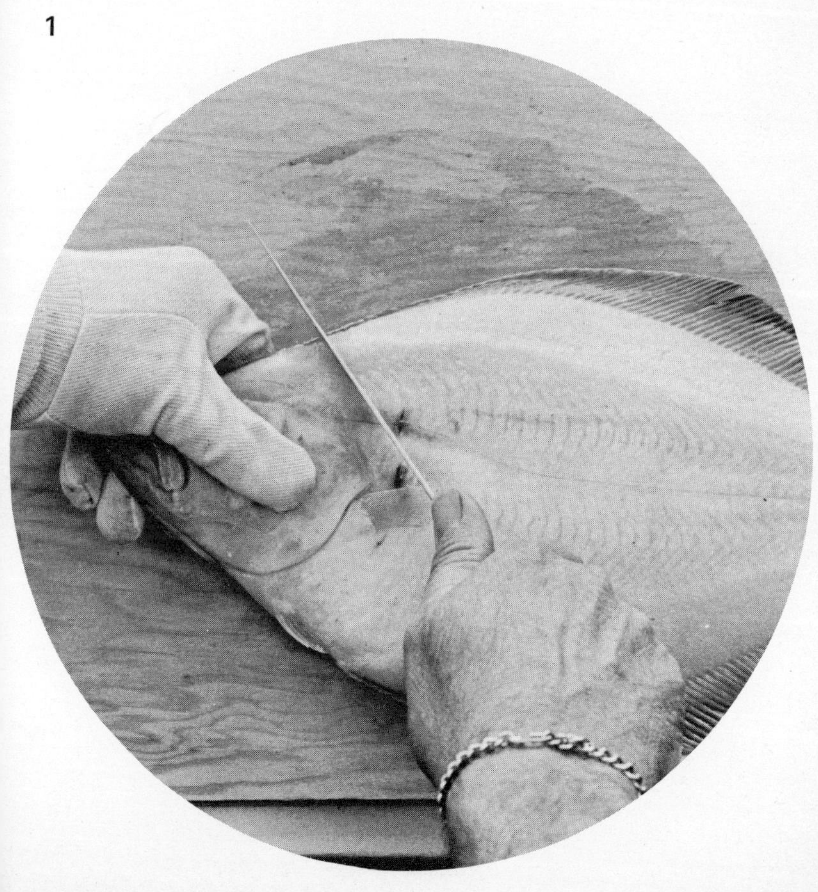

2/3/4. Turn the fish so the tail is nearly straight away from the working edge of the cutting board. The next cut is made with the knife inserted just to the right of the lateral line, a distinct series of scales showing as a line about midway from head to tail on the fish. With the knife held flat side up, insert the tip and make the thrust towards the tail, and at the same time cutting towards the edge of the fish. When making this cut, a slight downward pressure on the knife blade is necessary to keep the flat side of the knife gliding on the surface of the backbone.

2

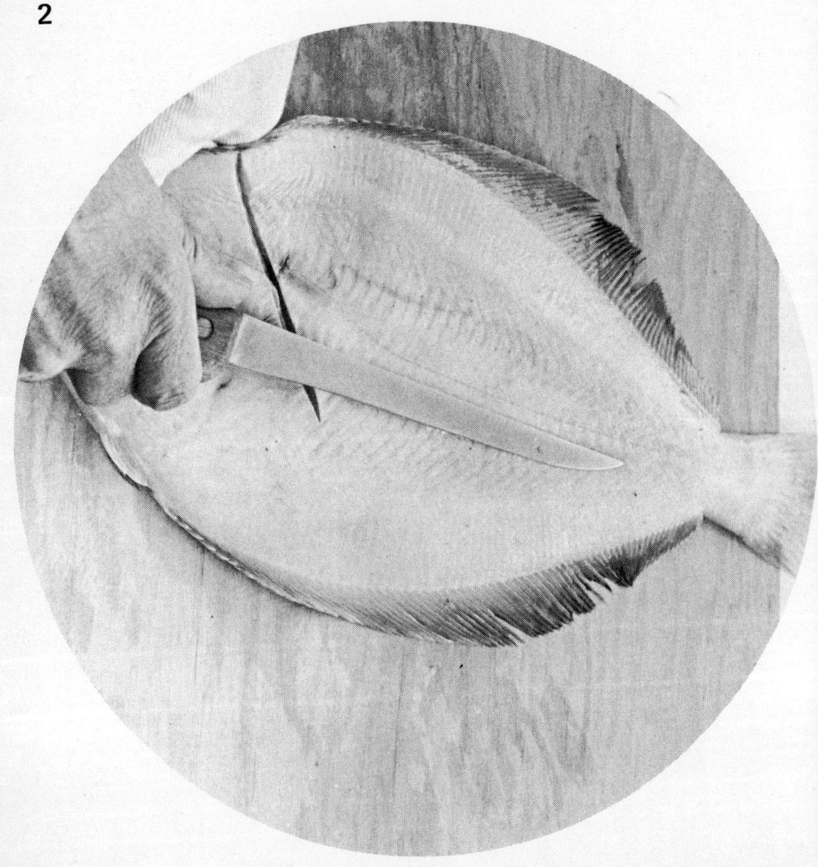

3

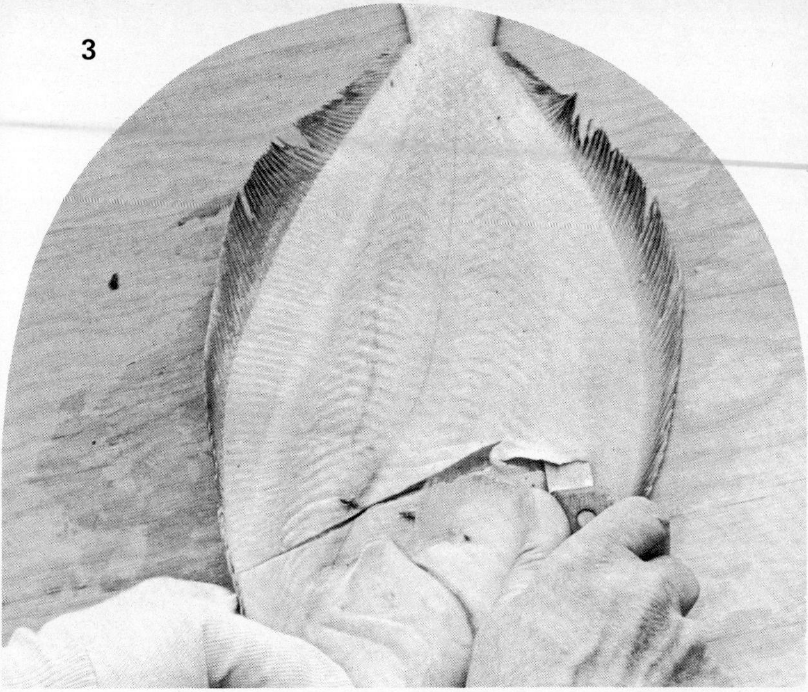

4

5/6. The third cut is made with the knife tip, starting from the tail end of the fillet. Hold up the cut part of the fillet and position the knife as shown (See 5). Exert enough downward pressure on the knife tip to make it bend and glide over the backbone, bring the cut forward to the head.

5

6

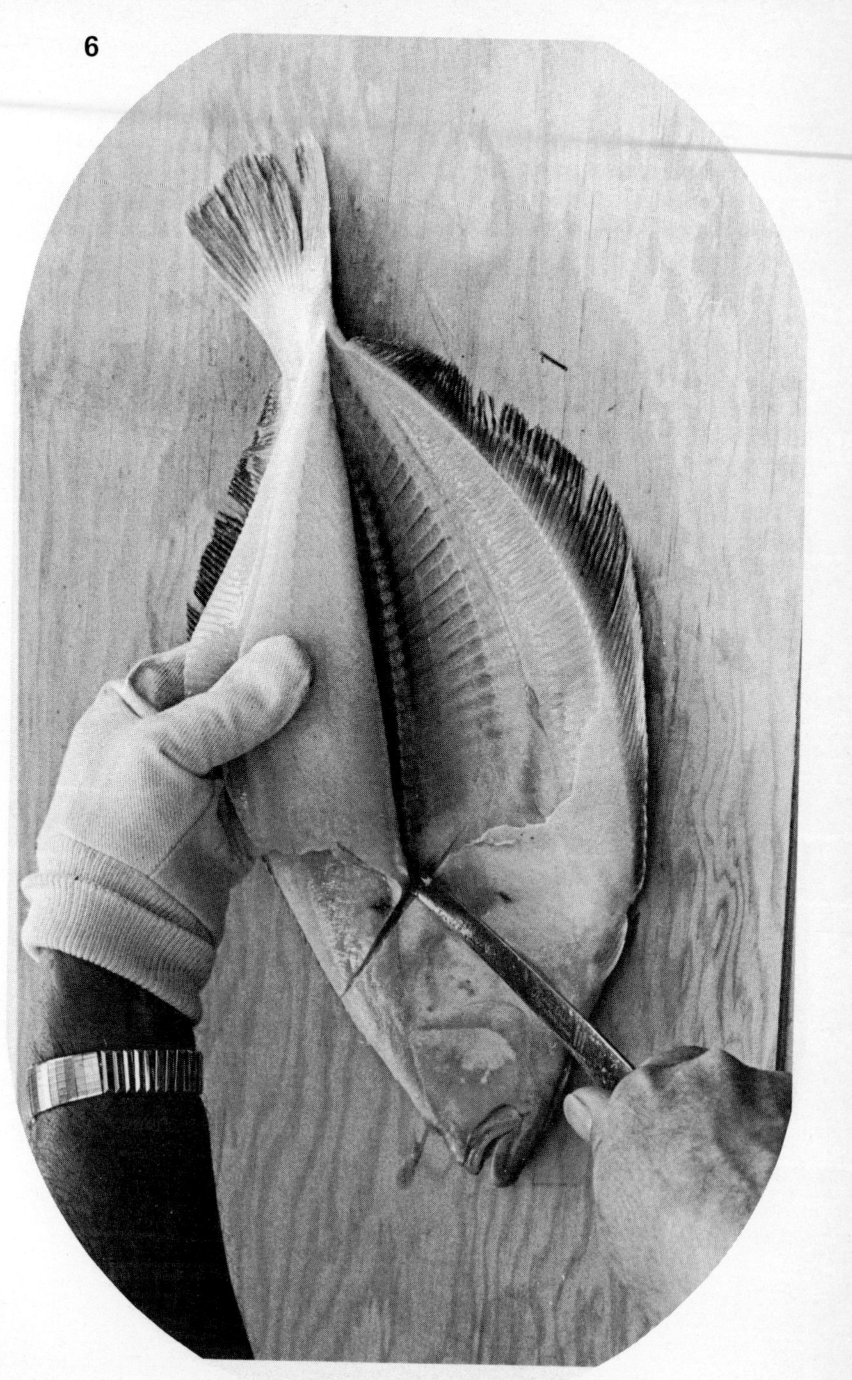

7/8/9. This cut removes the fillet from the fish. While holding up the cut portion of the fillet, start with the knife held flat in cut No. 1, cutting edge towards the tail. Exert a downward pressure to flex the knife blade to follow over the contour of the backbone, and cutting towards the tail, completely sever the fillet from the fish.

7

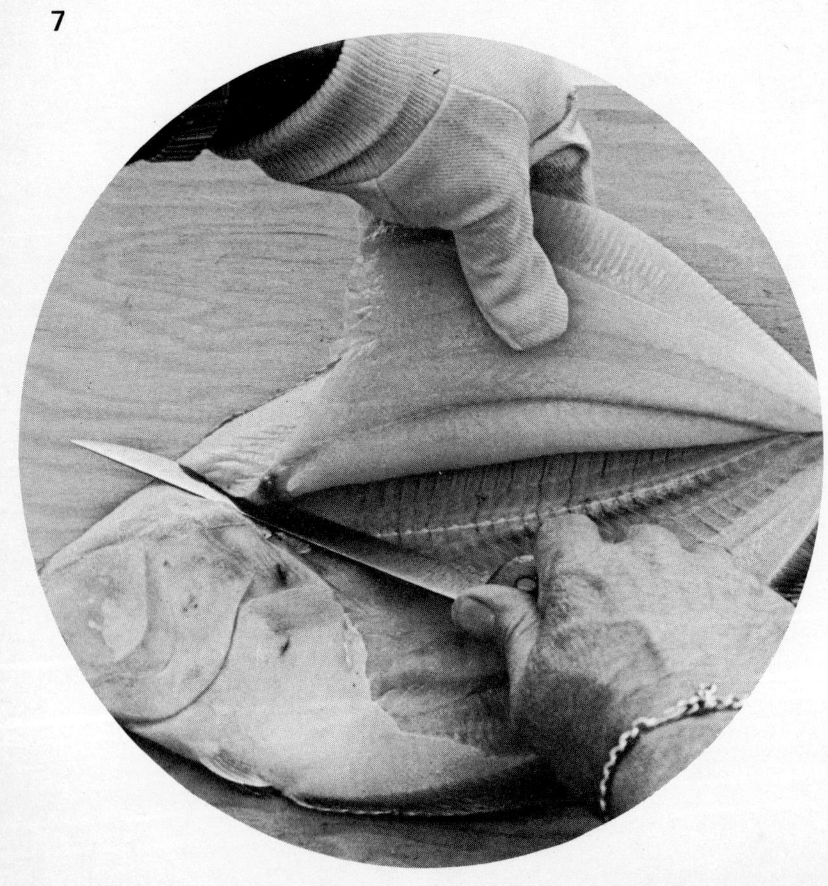

8

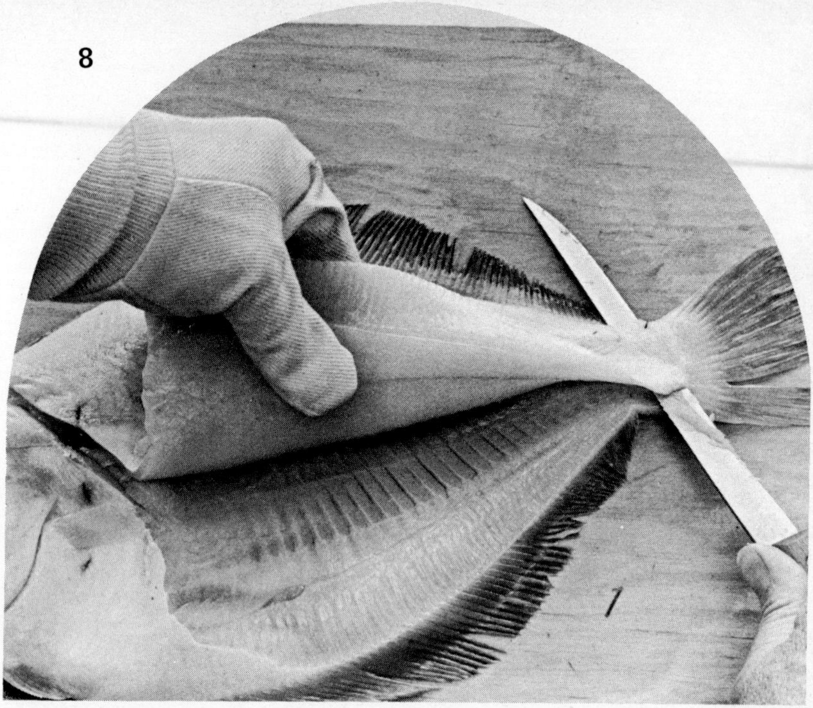

9

10/11/12. Now, turn the dark side of the fish up. The first cut on this side starts as a short, shallow, diagonal cut made in the thick, fleshy part directly in back of the head of the fish. Do not cut through the backbone. Next, insert the blade of the knife in this cut keeping the knife flat with cutting edge toward the tail. With a downward pressure on the blade to keep the flat side of the knife blade gliding over the backbone, cut to the end of the tail. Gauge the position of the knife tip so it will be following down the midline of the fish.

10

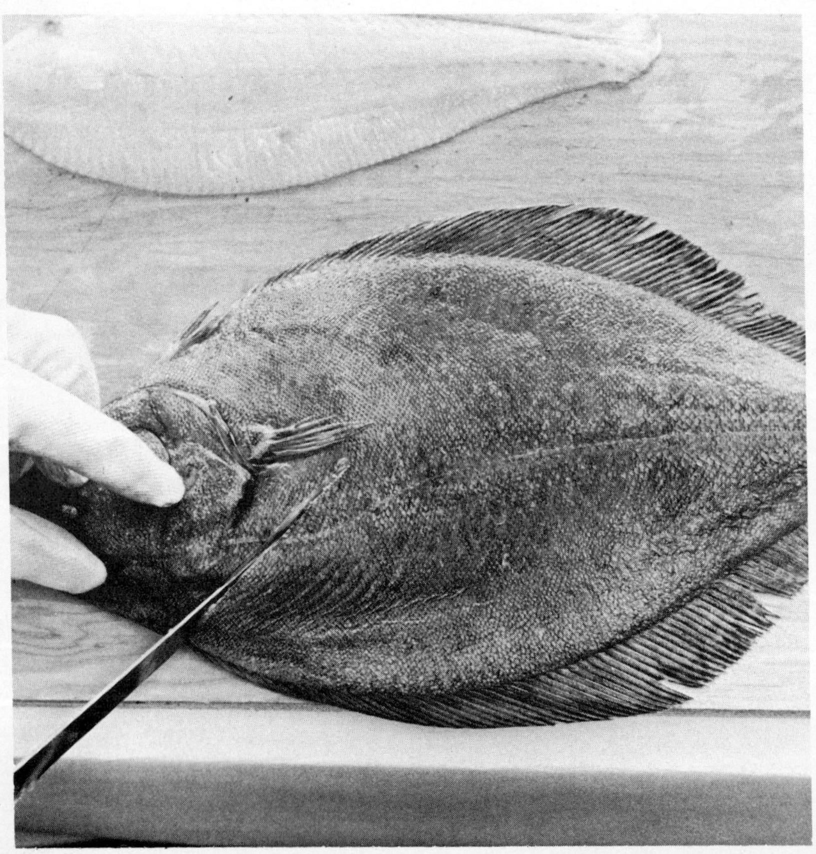

11

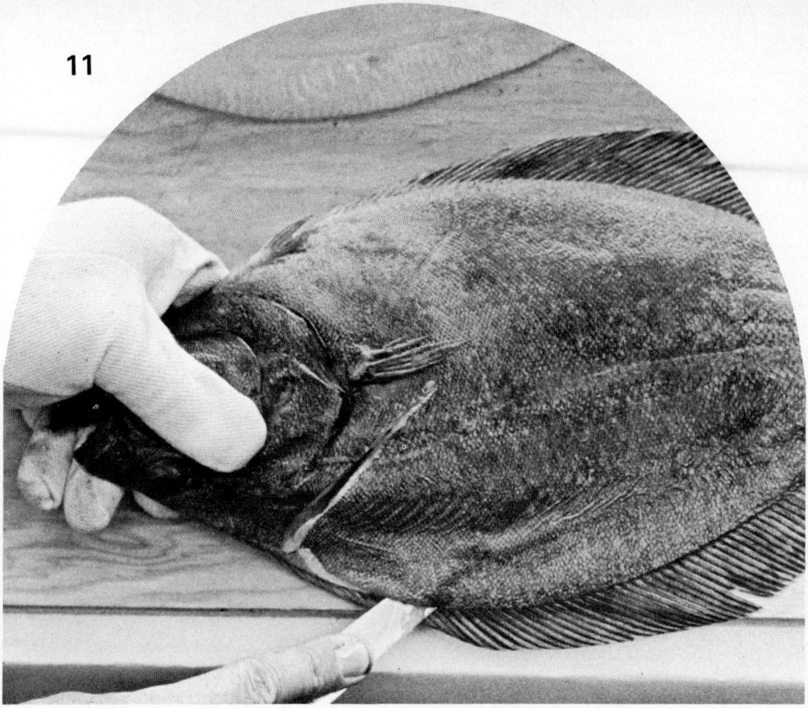

12

13/14. Start at the tail end of the fish. Hold up the cut part of the fillet, flex the knife tip down to allow it to glide over the backbone and over the rib bones as the cut is made, ending in back of the head. This cut should expose the stomach cavity.

13

14

15/16/17. This cut removes the dark side fillet from the fish. Hold the cut part of the fillet up. Cut behind the stomach cavity down to the backbone and out to the edge of the fish. Turn the knife so it lays flat on the backbone and complete the cut toward the tail, severing the fillet at the tail.

15

16

17

18/19/20. Now, remove the skin from the fillet. Position the fillet with the tail end toward the left. Cut through the flesh to the skin about one inch from the tail end of the fillet. Flatten the knife on the skin and remove the skin from the fillet by making a forward cut while holding the end of the skin down firmly on the board with the fingers. Repeat the same procedure to remove the skin from the other fillet.

18

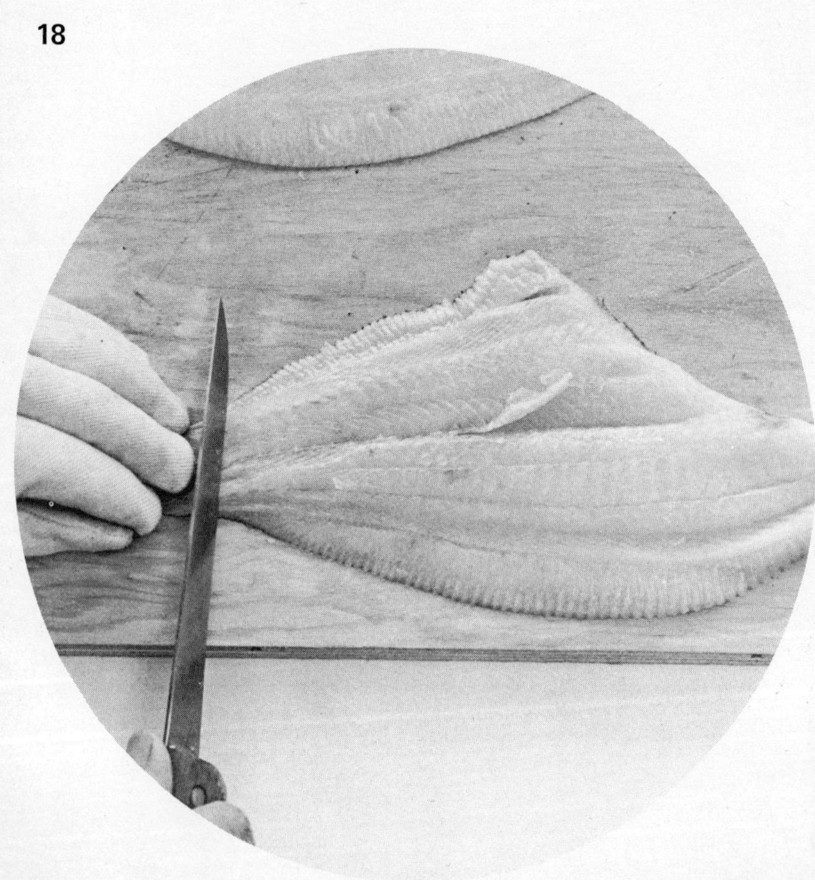

19

20

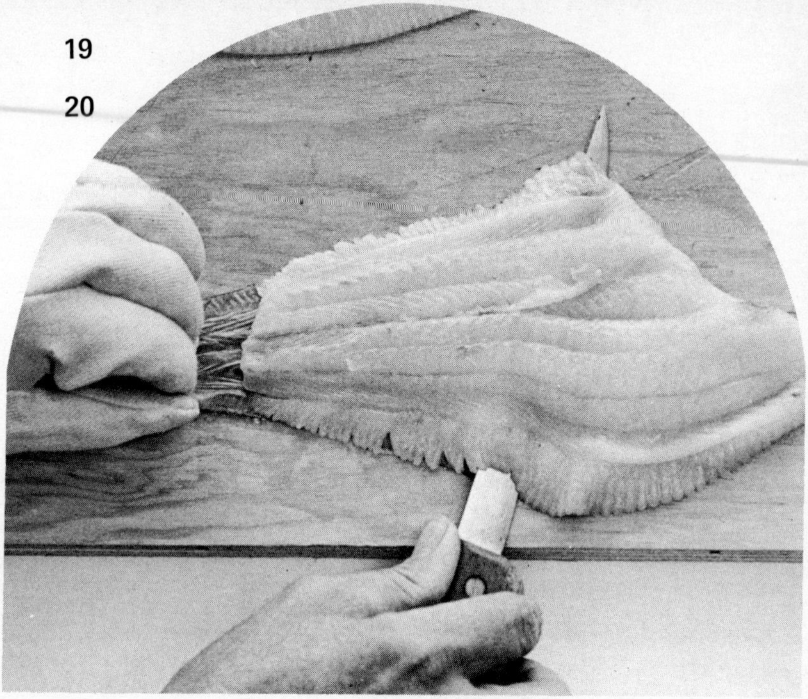

skinners

Skinners (Skinned, Whole Flounder)

Many flounders caught by salt-water anglers are too small to fillet, and can be best utilized by dressing and cooking them whole. Small flounders dressed in this manner are called "skinners."

1. With the white side of the fish up and head to the left, make one diagonal cut completely through the fish from the back of the head to the forward edge of the anal fin. This cut beheads and nearly eviscerates the fish.

2. Remove the tail in one single cut. Remove the anal fin with a cut starting from the tail end of the fish about ½ inch in from the edge of the fin and passing completely through the edge of the fish. Removal of the fin is easier if the cut is slightly angled in towards the body of the fish.

1

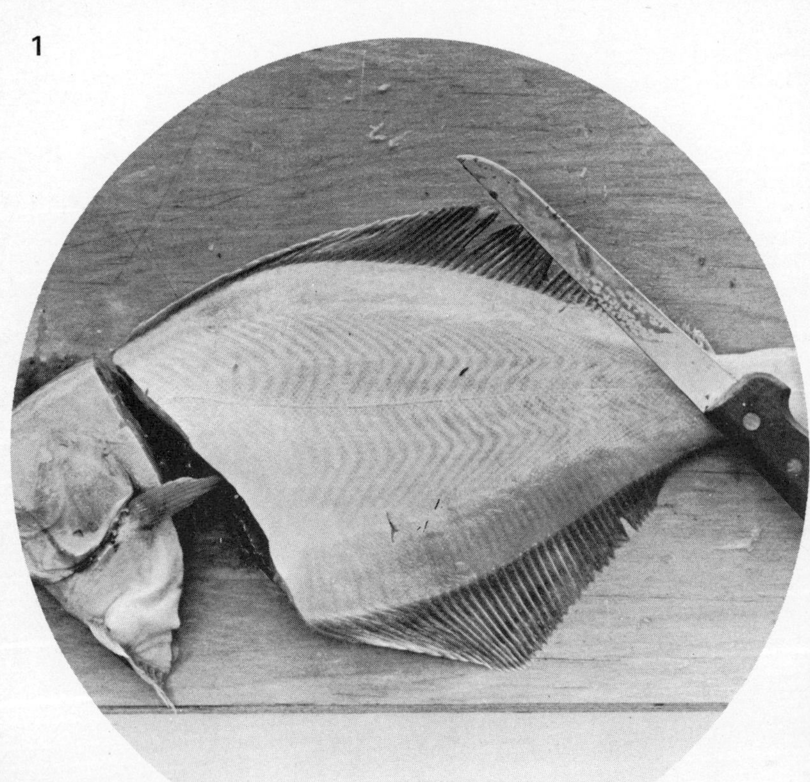

2

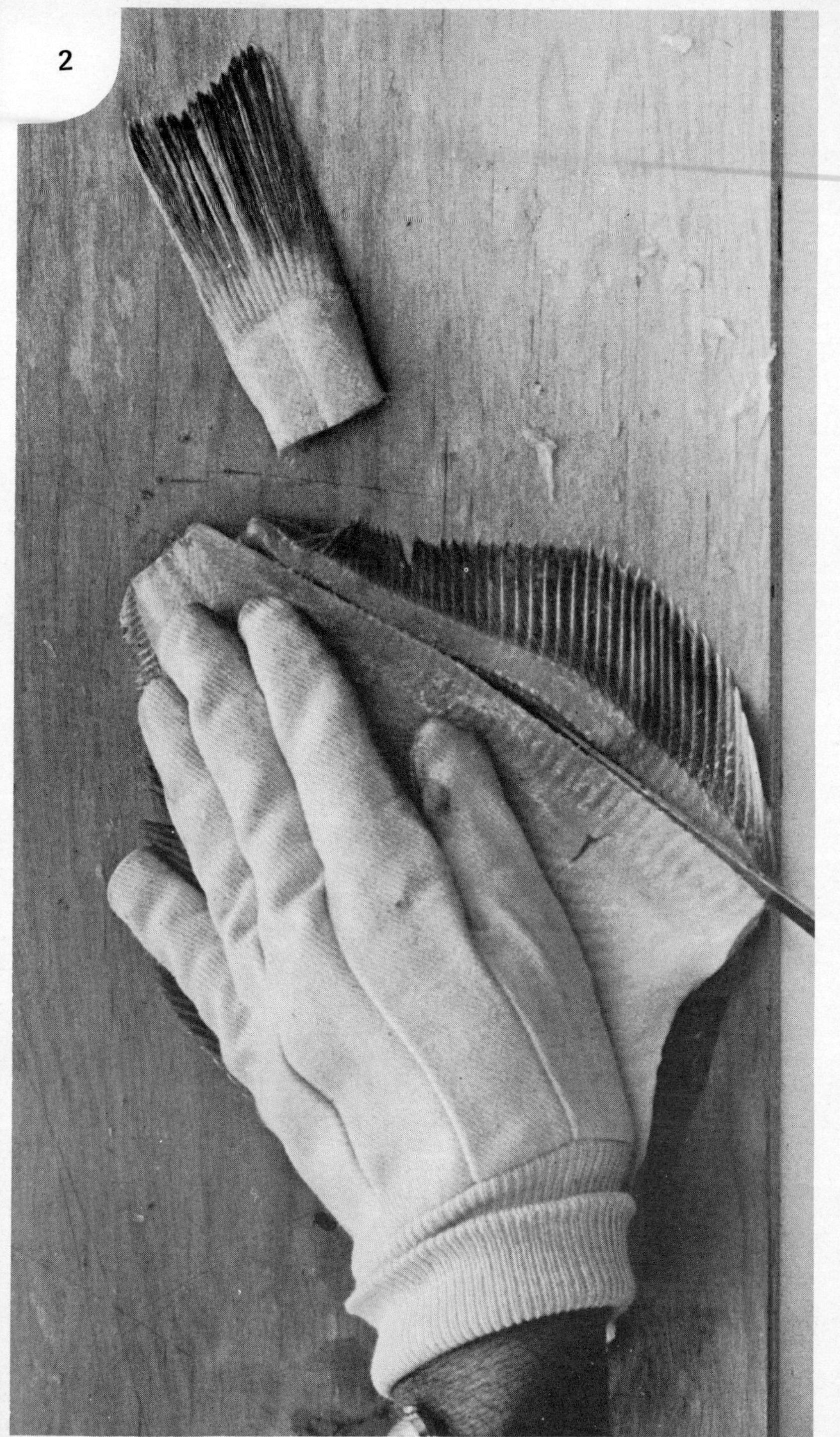

3/4. The cut removing the dorsal fin is the most important of all and needs to be made with care. This cut also permits removal of the dark skin on the eyed side of the fish. Start the cut at the forward end of the fish at a slight angle. Cut through the fin bones, but only down to the dark skin. Continue the cut to the end of the tail.

3

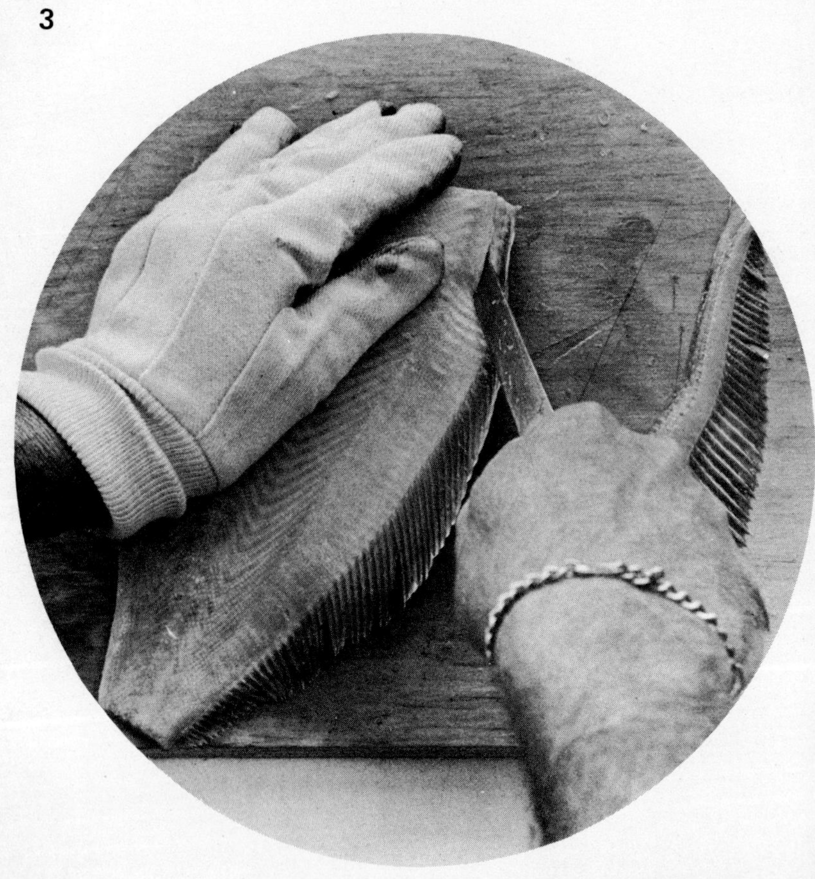

4

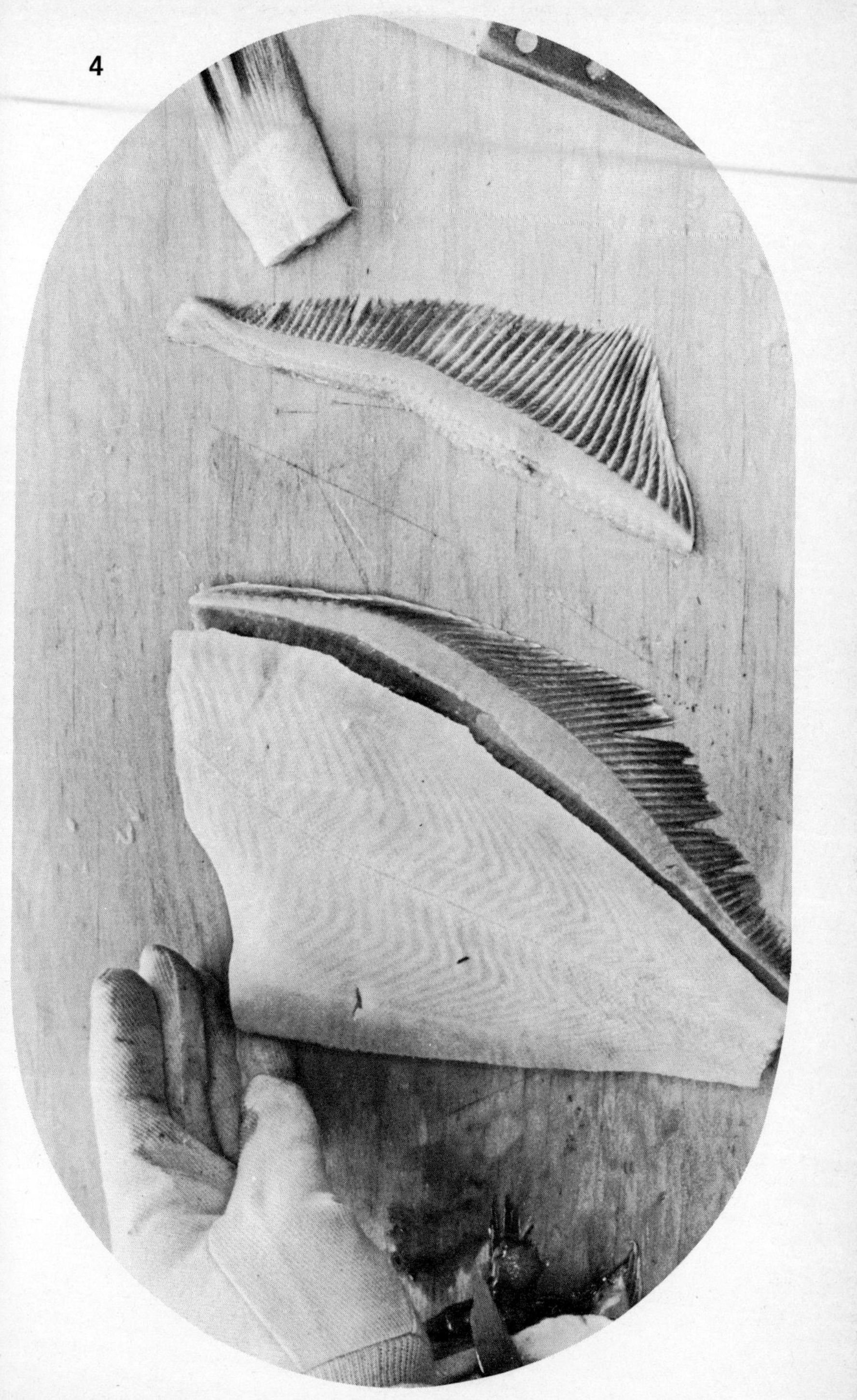

5/6. Start pulling the dark skin from the fish at the forward end. Get a good grip on both the body of the fish and the fin with the dark skin still attached and peel the dark skin from the fish. The fish is cooked with the white side skin attached.

5

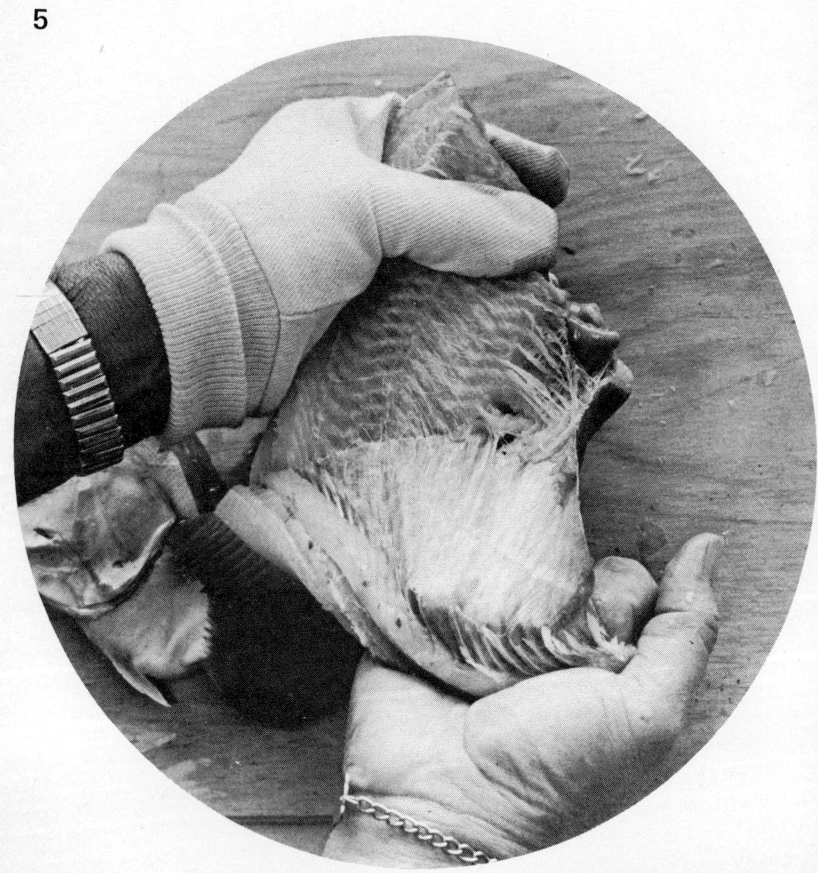

6

steaking

The following series of illustrations on making "steaks" from large flounder are presented to aid the person, who has some doubts about his filleting ability, in making the most use of his catch.

1/2. With the white side up and head to the left, start the cut through the thick, meaty part directly behind the head of the fish. Continue the cut through the backbone behind the stomach cavity, terminating at the forward end of the anal fin. This cut beheads and virtually eviscerates the fish. Next, follow the same procedures as in No. 2 through 5 for skinners in the previous section. This will remove the tail, anal, and dorsal fins and dark skin from the fish.

3. With the white side down, cut the fish into steaks of the desired width.

1

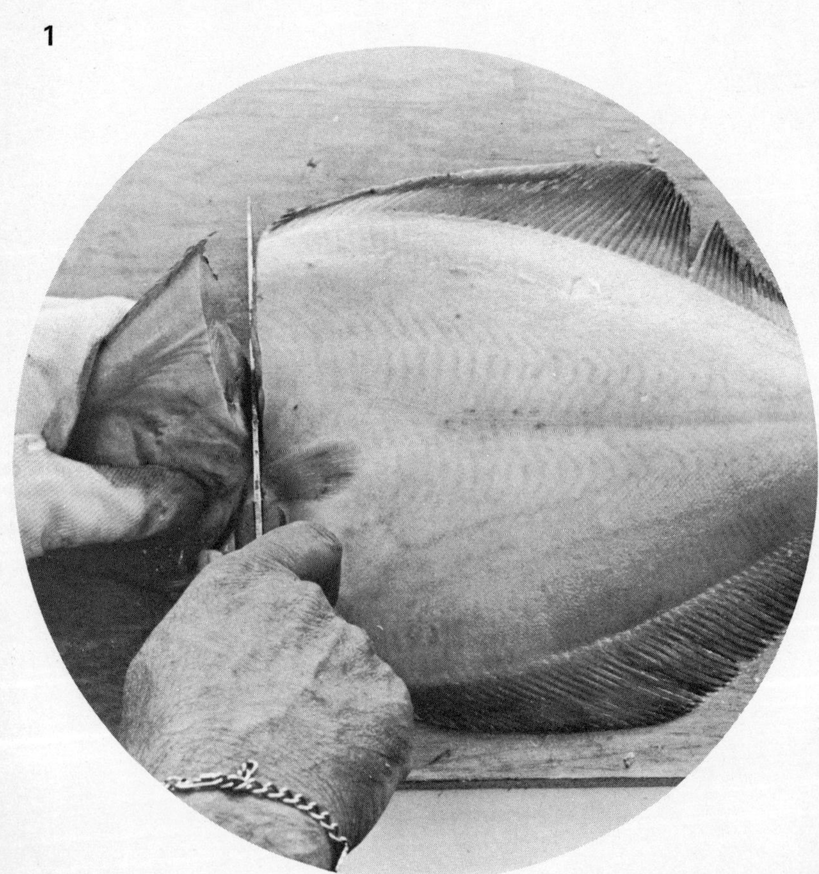

2

3

preparing roundfish

filleting

A salt-water catch will often include several varieties of fish such as lingcod and Pacific cod as well as several different species of rockfish. The filleting procedures for these remarkably different looking fishes are essentially the same. A rockfish is used in the following example as these fishes do present some special considerations. Even when rockfish are dead, the numerous head, dorsal and anal fin spines can painfully wound careless anglers. One of the easiest, quickest, and safest ways to remove the most edible portions of the rockfish is by filleting. A glove for handling the fish is recommended.

1. Lay the fish flat side down on the cutting board with the back to the working edge of the board and with the head on the right.

2. Start the first cut at an angle to the head as shown. Cut through the thick, fleshy part directly back of the head down to the backbone.

2

3/4/5. Turn the knife with the flat side up, insert the tip of the blade in the initial cut and cut towards the tail with the flat side of the knife gliding along the backbone. Keep a downward pressure on the knife blade, but do not cut too deep into the fish and sever the rib bones with the knife tip. As the cut is made towards the tail and the blade passes behind the stomach cavity, the blade can be thrust completely through the fish. Continue the cut to sever the fillet at the tail. In continuing the cut, flex the blade downward to allow it to glide over the backbone.

3

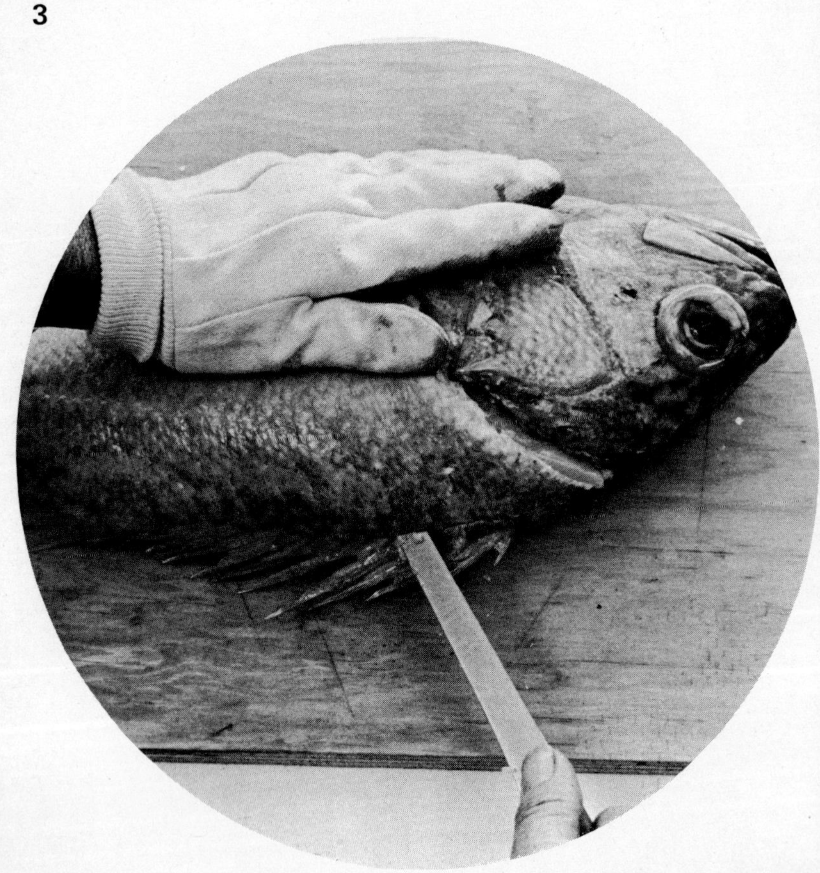

4

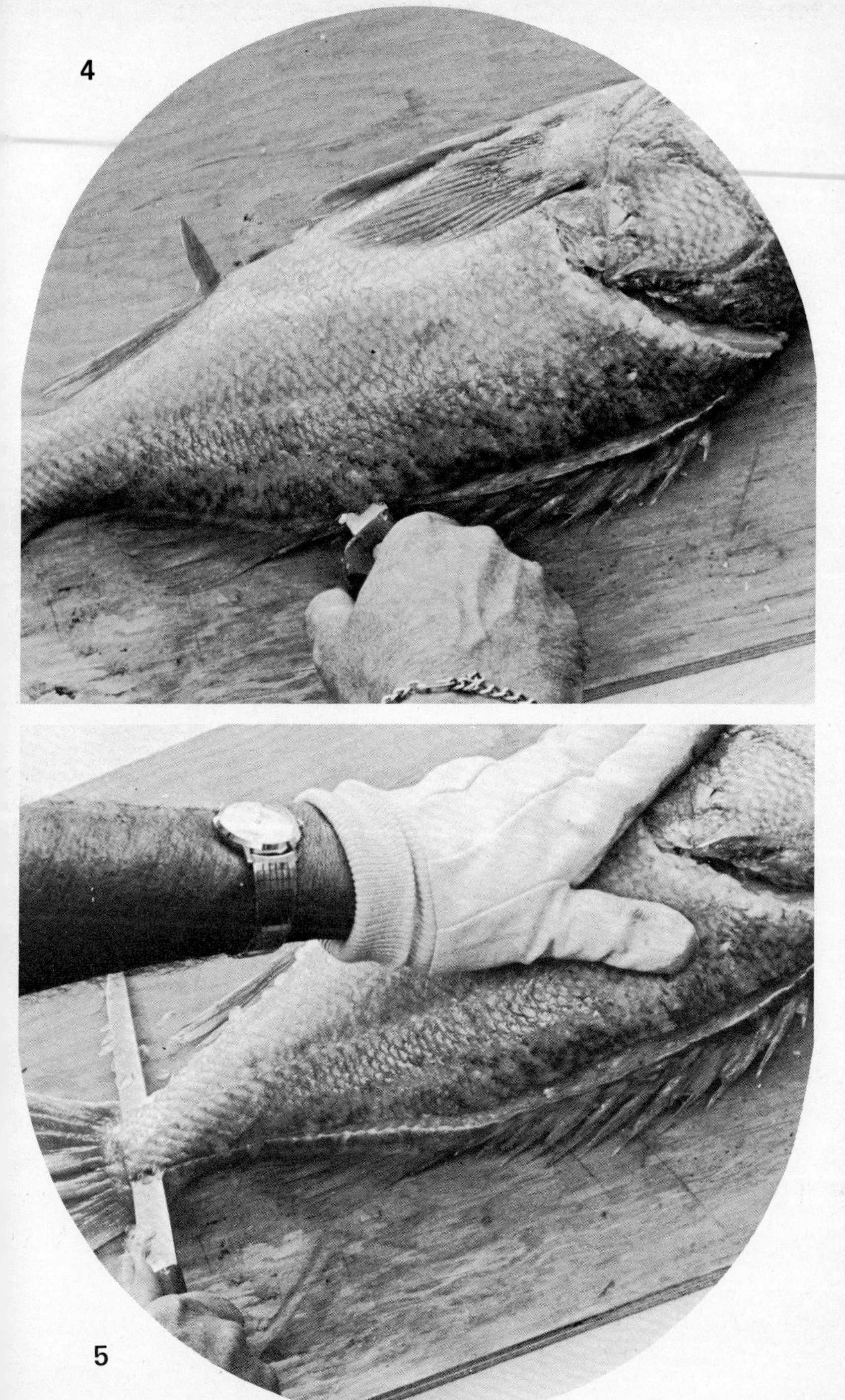

5

6. Hold up the partly severed fillet just behind the ribs and lay the knife blade flat on the backbone. As the cut is made towards the head, exert a

6

downward pressure to flex the blade so it will ride up and over the rib cage to end at the initial cut.

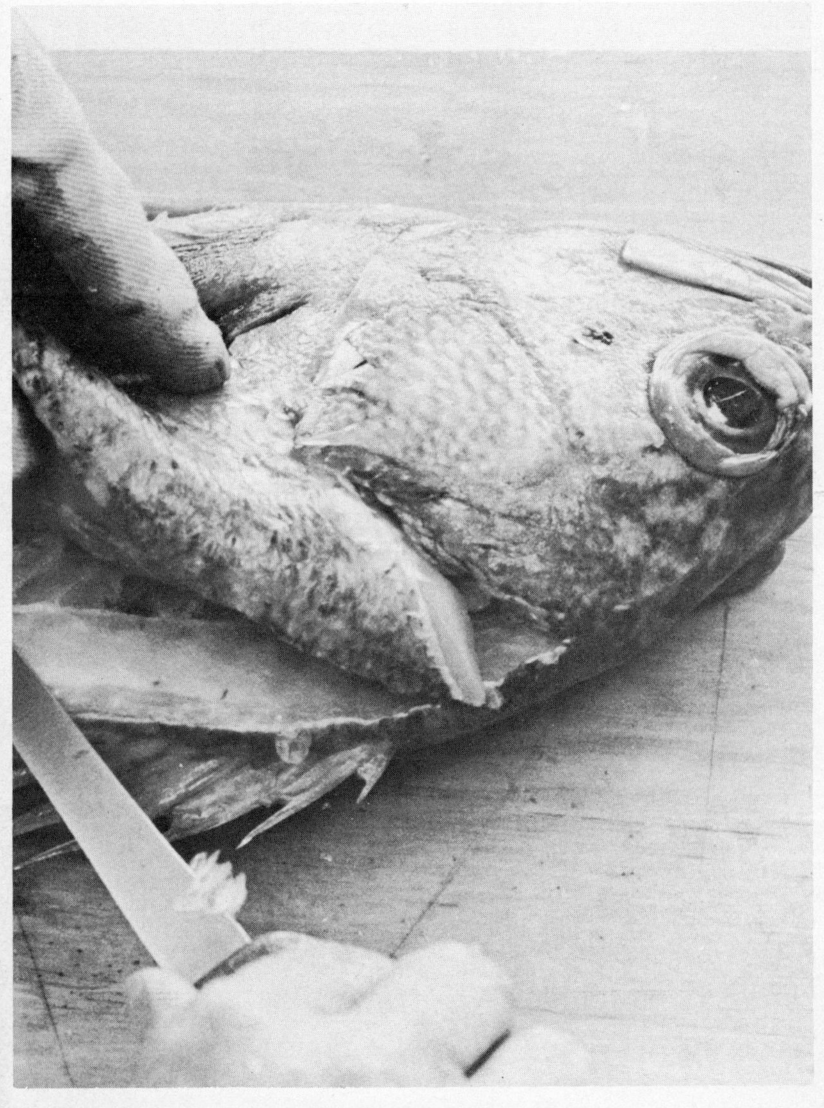

7/8/9. Hold the front part of the fillet up to start the final cut. Direct the line of cut down so the blade will slide over the ribs and the backbone to completely sever the fillet from the fish. Reverse the fish so that the head is to the left with the back to the working edge of the board. The procedures to remove the fillet from this side of the fish are the same as those just presented in No. 2 through 8.

7

8

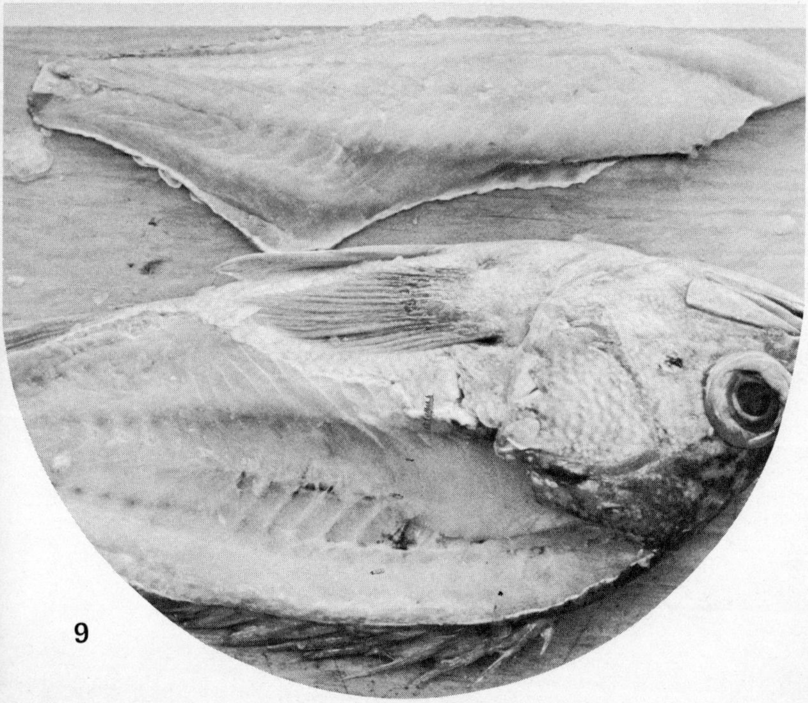

9

10/11/12. To remove the skin from the fillet, start at a point about one inch from the tail end of the fillet, cut through the flesh to the skin. The bit of flesh on the tail end of the fillet provides a grip on the skin while the flesh is being cut off. Hold the end of the skin down firmly, flatten the blade on the skin and separate the fillet from the skin by making a forward cut.

10

11

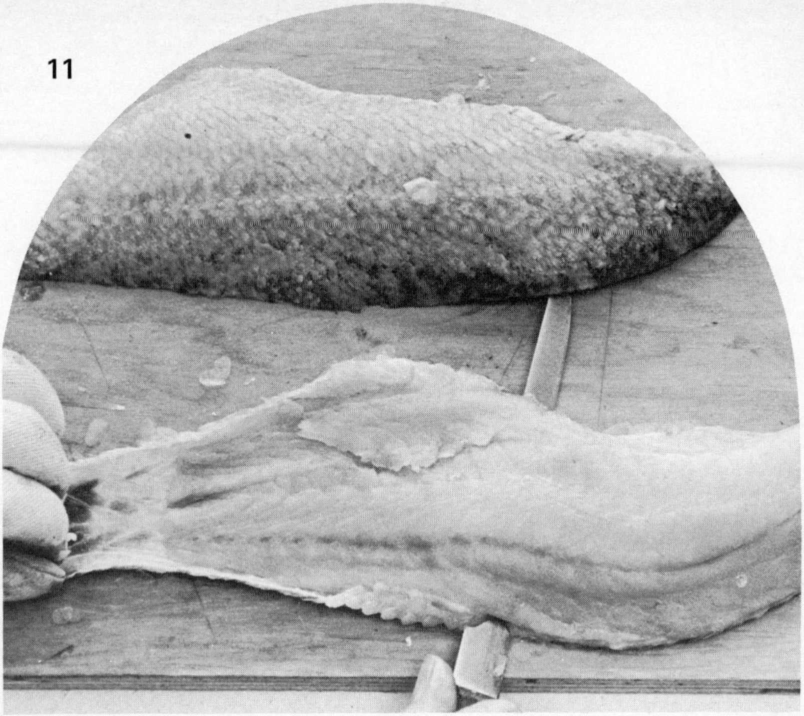

12

steaking

Any roundfish such as salmon, lingcod, Pacific cod, etc., can be steaked. In the following section, a lingcod is used as an example, but the procedures could be applied to most all roundfish. First, dress (eviscerate) fish and scrape out reddish kidney tissue remaining along the backbone in the stomach cavity. A spoon works well in removing the kidney tissue. Wash the fish thoroughly.

1. Cut the head off directly behind the pectoral fins.

2/3. Remove the fin (dorsal) on the back (Fish like lingcod have lone, spiny dorsals and their removal before steaking eliminates many bones from the steaks). Start the cut at the head end of the fish and cut about one inch deep along the full length. Repeat the cut along the other side of the fin and bring the two cuts together near the tail.

1

2

3

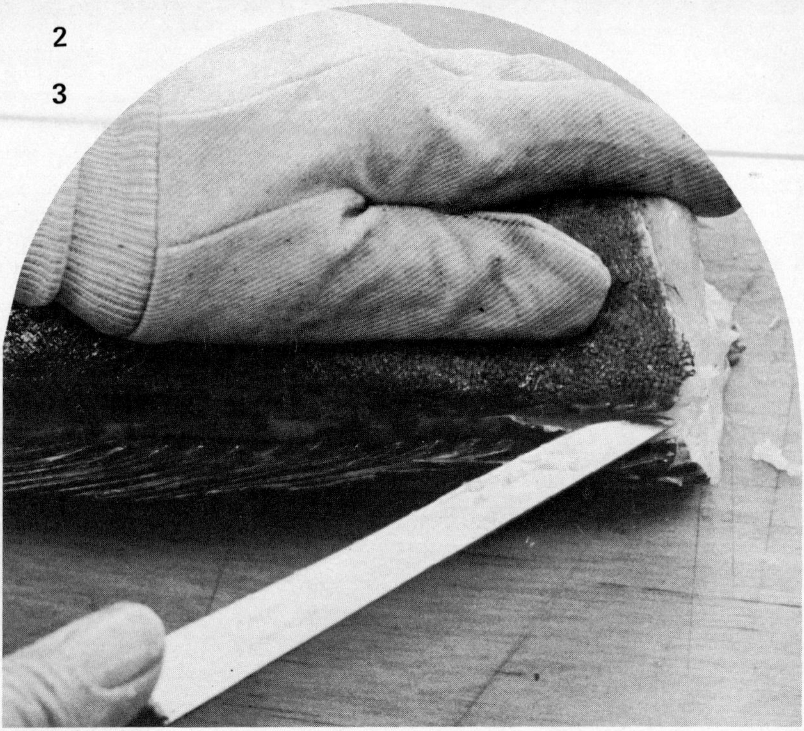

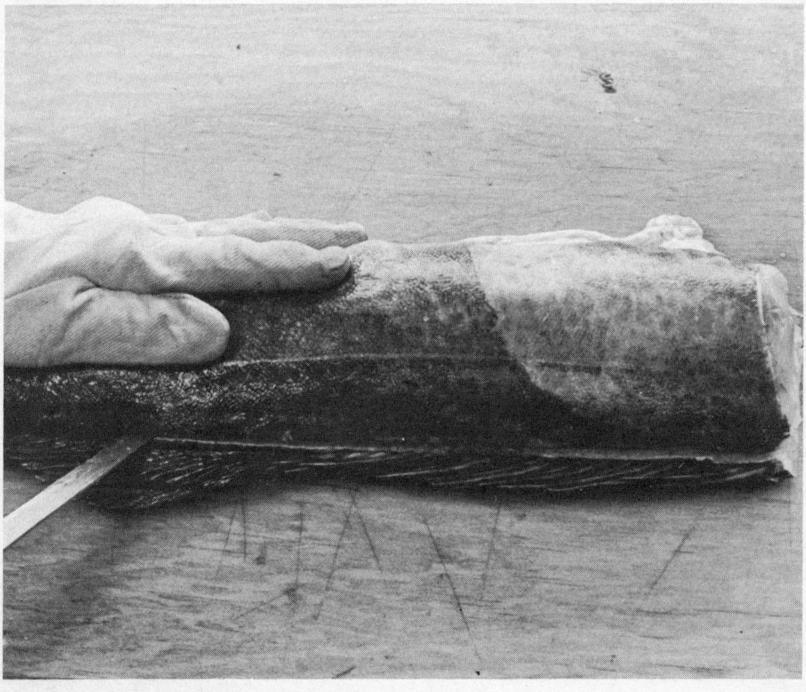

4/5. Grasp the tail end of the dorsal fin against the back side of knife and pull the fin completely out. Trim off the thin stomach wall if desired.

6. With a heavy knife, cut steaks about ½ inch to ¾ inch thick. A wooden block or mallet is often useful in hitting the backside of the knife to cut through the backbone of large fish. When the tail section of the fish becomes too small for steaking, two choice, boneless fillets can be cut from the remaining part of the fish. To remove the first fillet, insert the knife in the center top side of the tail section so that the flat side of the knife slides along the side of the backbone. Exert a downward pressure to keep the flat side of the knife riding the backbone and cut completely through to the groove left by removal of the dorsal fin.

4

6

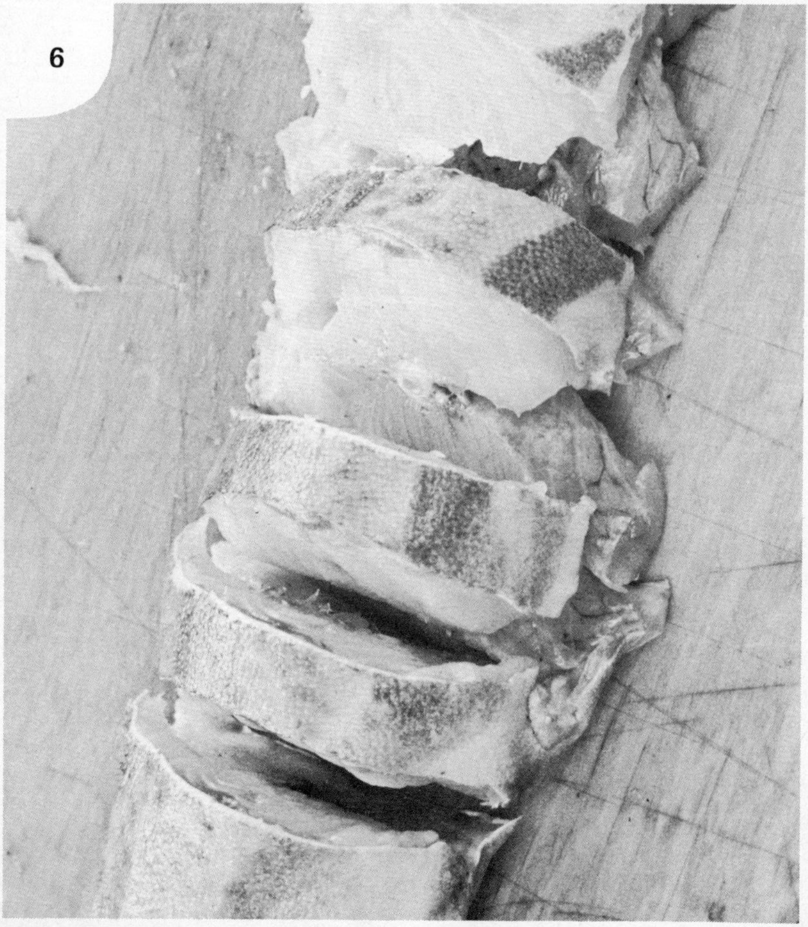

7. Hold the free edge of the fillet up to expose the backbone and with the flat edge of the knife following the backbone, cut in the opposite direction to free the fillet from the backbone.

8/9/10. Leaving the top fillet still attached to the tail section, hold the tail end with the gloved hand and cut through the flesh to the skin. Flatten the knife on the skin and cut the fillet away from the skin by pushing the knife forward.

7

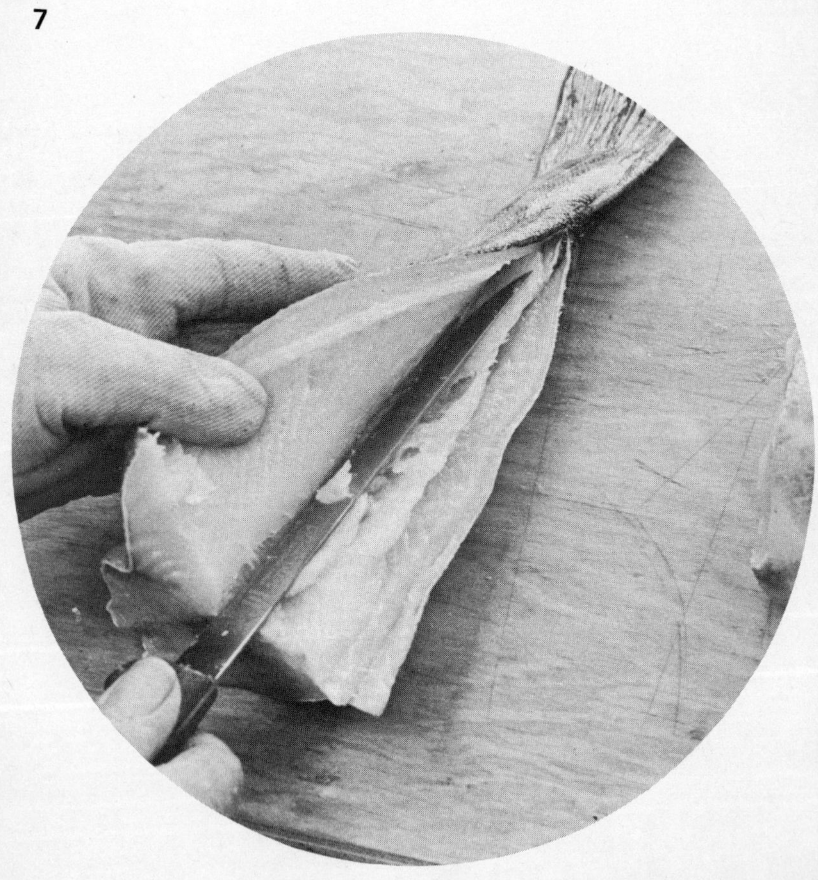

8

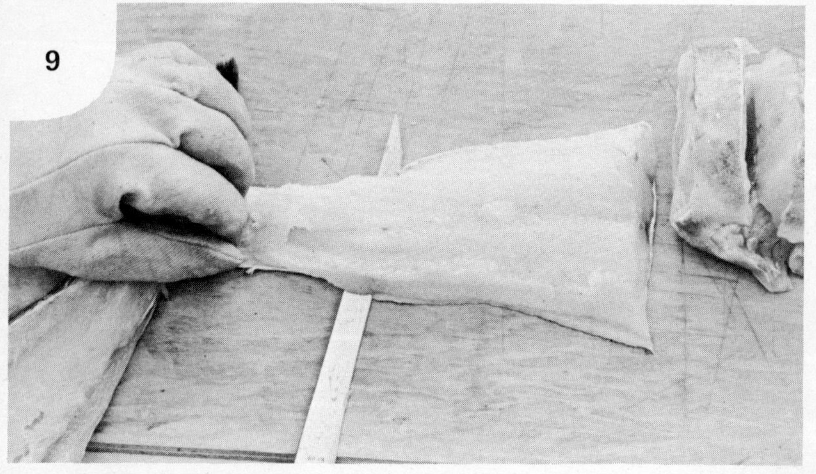
9

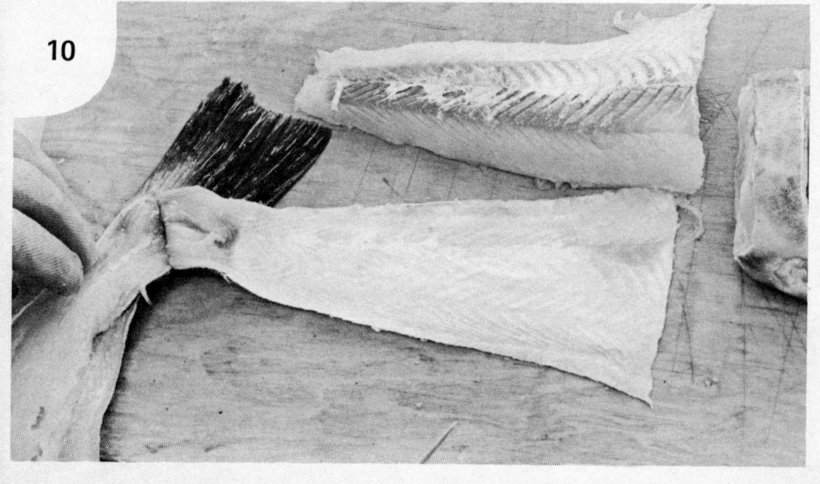
10

11/12. To remove the remaining fillet, insert the knife in the center and under the backbone of the remaining tail section. Continue the thrust so that the flat edge of the knife slides upward against the backbone. With the knife bearing against the backbone, cut to the edge to completely free the one side of the fillet from the backbone. Reverse the cut just described and cut the entire fillet away from the backbone. Remove the skin from this fillet as previously described in No. 9, 10, 11.

11

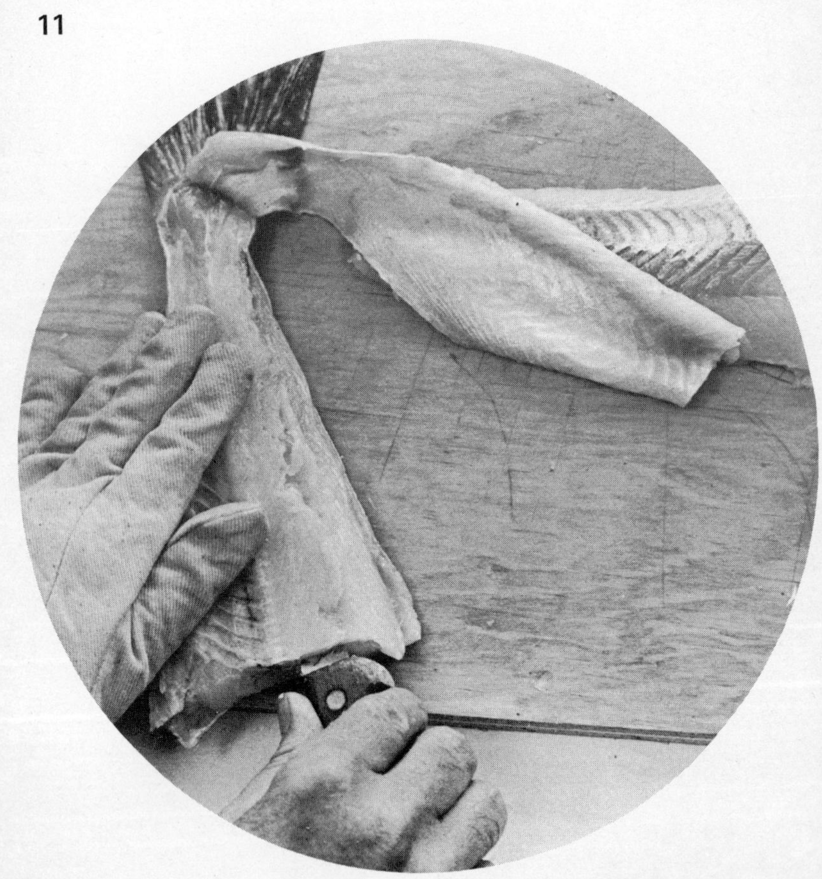

12

preparing salmon

The following procedures for dressing and making a salmon presentable for culinary preparation have been provided for the angler who is fortunate to catch one of the many salmon that abound in Washington waters, but is a bit apprehensive about this "do-it-yourself" task.

A fish can be dressed with head on or head off. The fins can be left on or cut off. For cooking, salmon can be steaked, following the instructions given in the section on steaking roundfish, used half or whole, and split or filleted with virtually all bones removed.

Since salmon are such a highly prized fish, a few hints on their care and cleaning are in order. Immediately upon landing a fish, kill it with a rap on the head with a small club to prevent it from bruising itself by flopping about. Bruises often cause "bloodshot" flesh which must be discarded. Always cool or ice-down your catch and dress the fish as soon as possible. Leaving the entrails in a fish for an extended time, especially during warm weather, will cause "belly burn" to take place inside the fish. This situation is more prevalent in heavily feeding salmon.

If desired, salmon scales can be easily removed with water pressure from a garden hose, provided they haven't been allowed to dry. By directing the water flow from tail to head, a "bright" fish can be descaled in a matter of seconds. If plans call for steaking a salmon after it is dressed, cut off the tail and locate the small blood vessel directly below the vertebrae (backbone). With moderate water pressure, apply the end of the hose directly onto this area, forcing the blood contained in the vessel out into the rear portion of the body cavity. This trick will leave steaks blood free when they are cut. Descaling before cutting also helps give scale-free, attractive steaks.

1/2/3. Starting from the vent (anus), cut through the stomach wall forward toward the head to expose the entrails, ending the cut just past the pectoral fins.

1

2

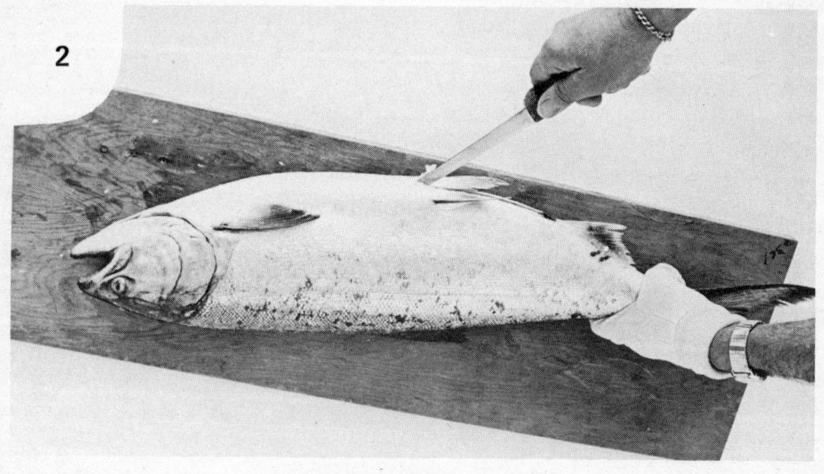

3

4/5/6/7/8/9. Grasp the gills firmly and cut through the narrow triangular part of the "throat". Continue the cut to sever the gills from the body, while pulling the gills away from the cut. Cut away the gills.

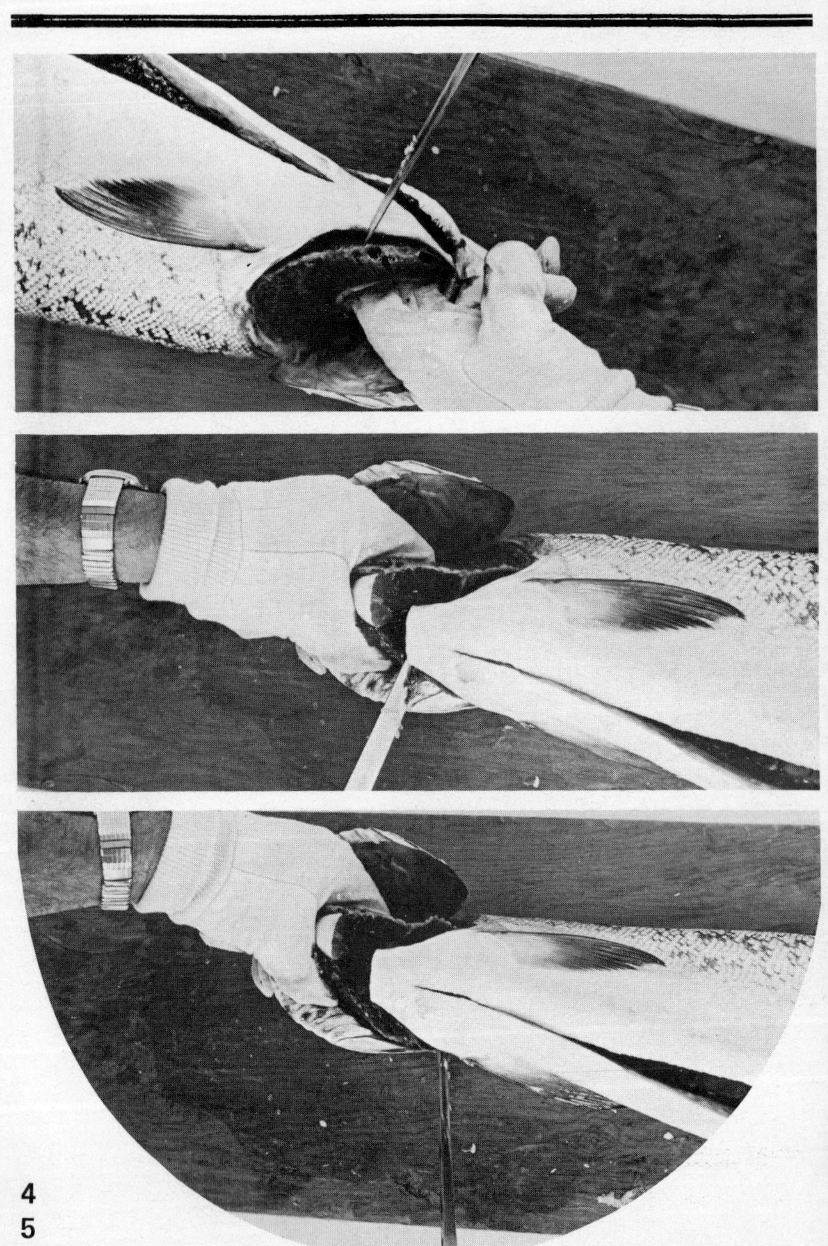

4
5
6

7
8
9

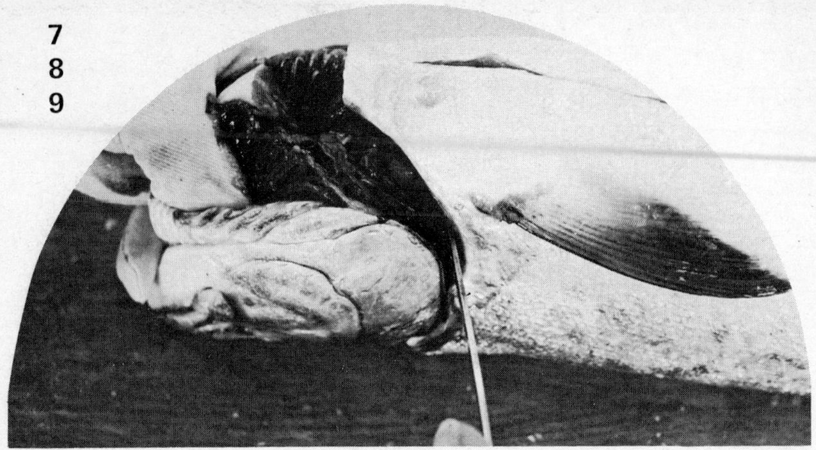

10. Cut the membranes which attach the gullet to the sides of the body wall, cutting completely around as close to the body wall as possible. Grasp the gullet with attached organs and, while pulling towards the tail, remove the entire visceral mass.

11/12/13. The kidney lies along the backbone and appears as a whitish, tapered membrane. This membrane must be cut to remove the kidney — a dark, blood-colored mass. The cut may be directly down the middle, or on either side of the kidney, just inside its attachment to the ribs. The extra cut will allow for complete removal of the membrane and gives a neater appearance to the body cavity of a dressed fish.

10

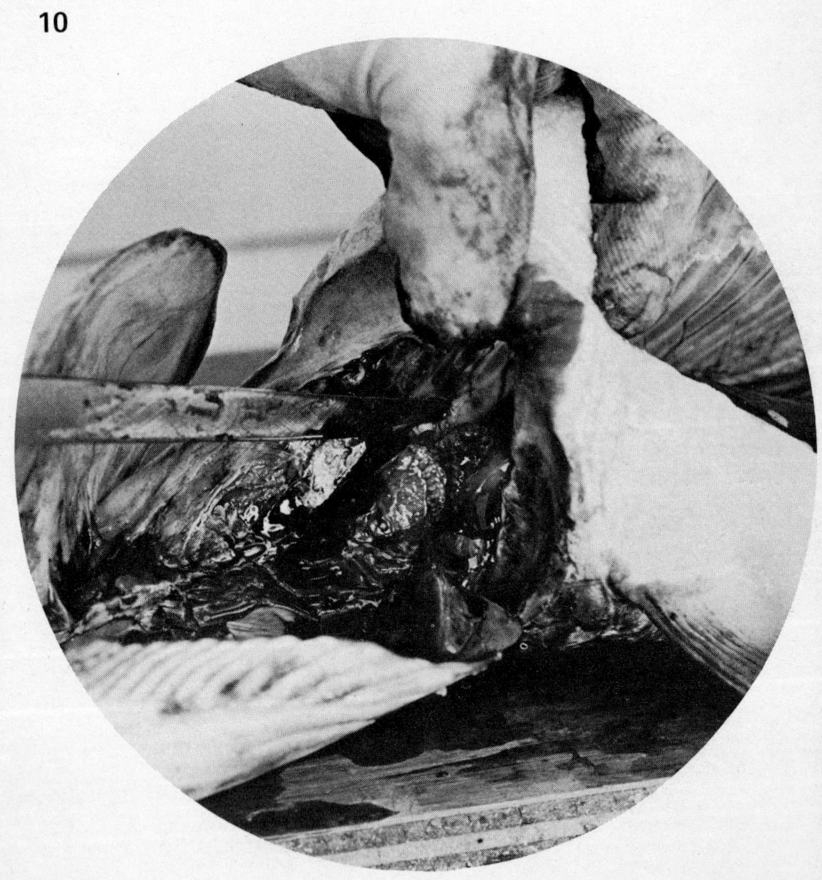

11
12
13

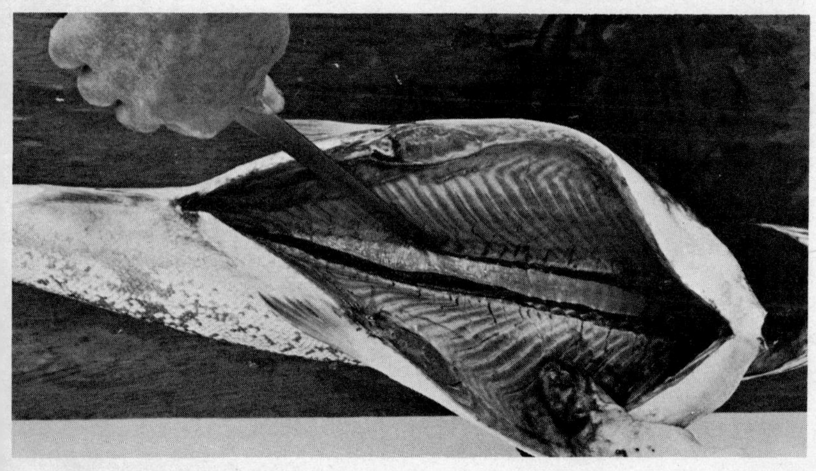

14/15/16/17. Working from head to tail, scrape out the membrane and kidney with a tablespoon. Scrape the area, where ribs join the backbone, vigorously with the tip of the spoon to remove any traces of blood. Wash the body cavity thoroughly and scrape away all remaining tissues to complete the operation for a dressed fish with head on.

14

15
16
17

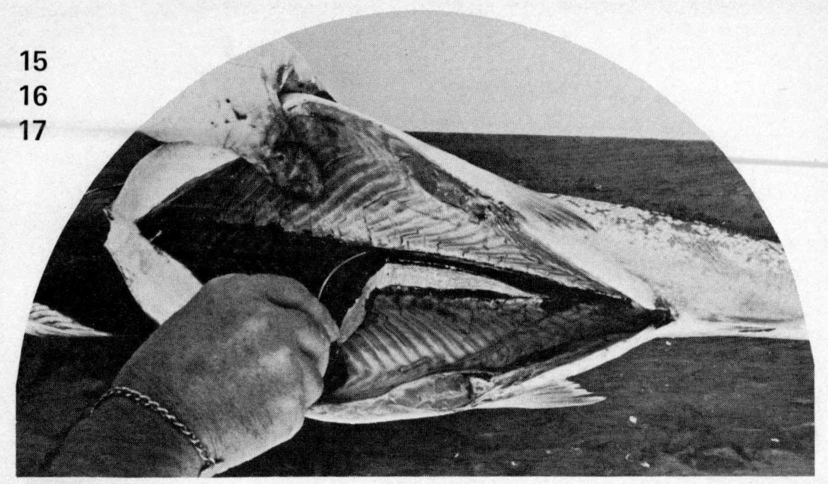

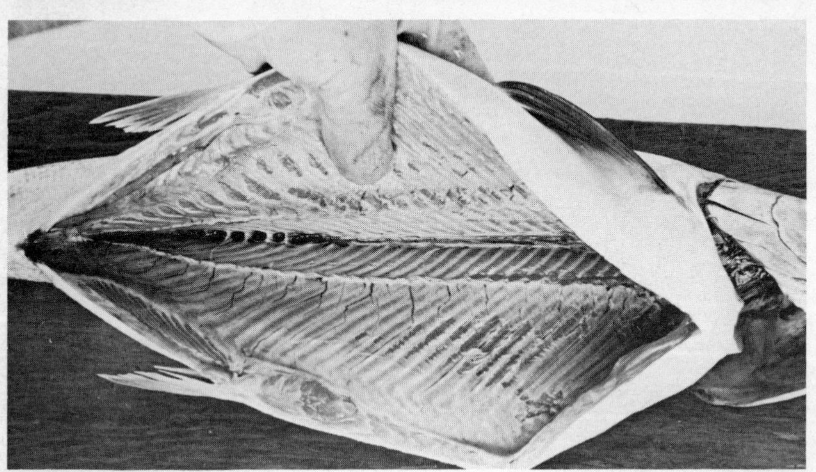

18. To dress the fish, head off, follow the curved contour of the forward part of the fish and cut away the head.

19/20/21/22. Fin removal is optional. This chore requires a very sharp knife. For easier fin removal, cut slightly below the point of fin attachment. If fin removal is desired, doing so before dressing out the fish is much easier, especially when cutting off the pelvic and pectoral (belly) fins. These should be removed with a quick, forward thrust of the knife, but use caution!

18

19
20
21
22

filleting

23/24/25. To fillet the salmon, start with the fish dressed, head off. Continue the cut shown in No. 7 to completely sever the remaining attachment of the body walls (at the throat). To remove the first (top) fillet, start the cut at the "head end" of the fish, directly above the backbone (similar to the cut shown in No. 26 for the second fillet). Cut towards the tail, holding the knife flat and firmly against the backbone and, while making this cut, let the knife protrude so that it can be kept following down the center of the back of the fish.

Continue through to the end of the tail.

23

24

25

26/27/28/29/30/31/32. A bit of practice is required to remove the backbone in one cut. These procedures are for the novice, who should use several cuts to remove the backbone and its connected bones without losing too much flesh. With the tip of the knife, start cutting through the ribs at the head end of the fish, keeping the knife's cutting edge always up, toward the backbone. Continue the cut to the end of the body cavity, then cut to the end of the tail. Always keep the cutting edge of the knife gliding along the bones. Continue cutting the backbone from the flesh until the backbone is free.

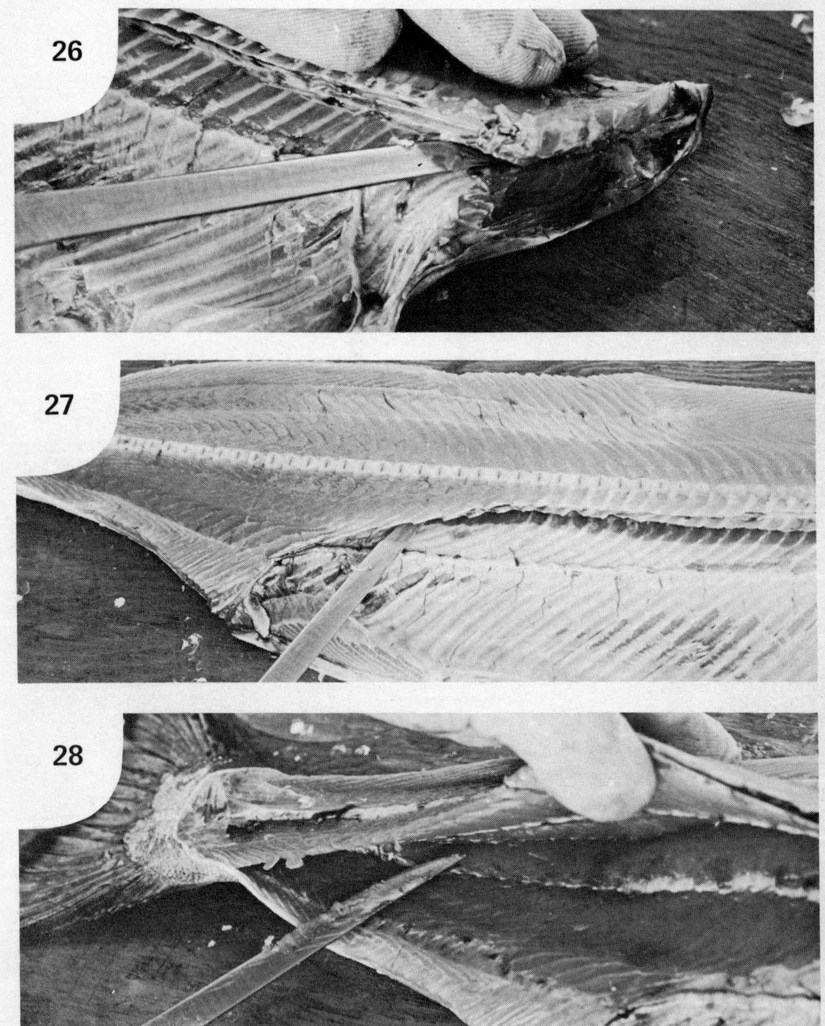
26

27

28

29

30

31

32

33/34/35/36. Remove the ribs from each fillet by cutting under the ribs with the knife's edge against the bones. Flex the knife downward to follow the rib contour.

33

34
35

36

WINSOR

about the authors...

Frank Haw has been a biologist with the Washington Department of Fisheries since 1959. He was born in Seattle, Washington in 1932 where he attended Franklin High School. Utilizing a "G.I. Scholarship", he received his Bachelor of Science degree in Fisheries from the University of Washington, College of Fisheries in 1959. Joining the Department of Fisheries staff, Mr. Haw began work on the Sport Fishery and was promoted to Project Leader of this section in 1963.

Mr. Haw's avid interest in sport fishing goes back to his early years. Now married with three children, this interest persists and has had a strong influence on his professional efforts to enhance the recreational fisheries in Washington.

Raymond M. Buckley has been a biologist on the Sport Fishery staff of the Washington Department of Fisheries since 1964. He was born in Sedro Woolley, Washington in 1940 and spent most of his young adult life in Seattle. He received his Bachelor of Science degree in Marine Fisheries Biology from the University of Washington, College of Fisheries in 1963. After a year of graduate work at the University of Hawaii, he returned to Washington and joined the Department of Fisheries staff. With Department sponsorship, he received his Master of Science degree in Fisheries from the University of Washington in 1969.

Mr. Buckley is an avid marine sport fisherman and has spent most of his professional career working to improve the recreational use of Washington's marine waters.